THEY AIN'T GONNA GET ANY DEADER

by Greg Dorchak

Austin, Texas

They Ain't Gonna Get Any Deader

Author's note: the stories related herein are true, perhaps slightly exaggerated
in places, underplayed in others. Some names of people or places may have
been changed out of respect, memory loss, or because it was funnier.

Inquiries should be addressed to:
greg@classclownpictures.com

ISBN-13: 979-8-3302-3651-0
US Copyright Registration: TXu 2-438-474
Library of Congress Control Number: 2024916016

Edited by Nicole Zayas-Dorchak
Interior and cover design by Greg Dorchak
Photo on page 253 by Carmen Zayas

Printed in the United States

*mended for anyone who loves heartfelt stories and
the magic of small-town living... the stories were just
right, with a touch of David Sedaris flair."*

(Of Pigs And Meteorites)
-- Bill Boyea
Web Application Developer

*"For anyone who grew up in rural America, the
stories and memories will immediately reconnect you
with your own misadventures and misunderstandings
of youth in wide open spaces. Although it strives to
be silly and irreverent (and does a damn fine job of
it), there is still a feeling the writer maintains a high
regard for the location of his upbringing and a feeling
these moments are sacred in influencing his view of
people and the world around him."*

(Of Pigs And Meteorites)
-- Marc Isaacs
Writer/producer, film industry

*"Of Pigs and Meteorites" is not merely a collection of
anecdotes; it is a journey into the heart of nostalgia,
a narrative that bridges the gap between past and
present with a genuine sense of humanity. Dorchak's
recollections serve as a testament to the enduring
power of place and the profound impact it can have
on shaping one's character."*

(Of Pigs And Meteorites)
-- Grace Jackson

*"...this has been both (1) a disarming, plainspeaking,
literally laugh-out-loud affair, and (2) something I
can't help but wish I'd had by my side years and years
ago... practical nuts and bolts and frank realities
that are hard to have much of an idea about without
getting boots on the ground -- but not in any sort*

*of gatekeeping, scared-straight, "Reefer Madness"
sense. I expect this little aptly named guide would
go a certain distance toward helping the beginning
actor feel less in the weeds and hopelessly out of place
when people start talking about the business end of
things"*

(Good Shit To Know About Being A Film Actor)
-- Brian Villalobos
Actor

*"One of the most outstanding children's books ever
written, it is so helpful to parents. I just finished
reading it and thought how much it could help
children who are scared at night. Children are told,
"There is no such thing as monsters." Instead, they
have a parent who defends them and helps their child
sleep better and feel protected at night."*

(Where Monsters go When You Grow Up)
-- Sandy Turmail

*"What fun for a youngster to read this story and fig-
ure out how the father gets tricked in the end. It is of
a level that young readers can see the trick developing
and surely this helps kids develop their understanding of irony and perhaps a bit about hypocrisy, but in
such a subtle, fun way."*

(Who took My Crayons?!)
-- Tiger Anderson

Other books by Greg Dorchak:

Three More Screenplays by Greg Dorchak

Three Screenplays by Greg Dorchak

Of Pigs And Meteorites

Good Shit To Know About Being A Film Actor

How To Pull A Movie Out Of Your Ass

Who Took My Crayons?!

Where Monsters Go When You Grow Up

For Tabb High
Class of 1982
GO TIGERS!

Contents

They Ain't Gonna Get Any Deader

THE CHOSEN ONE

Texas has Fire Ants. Fire Ants – pardon my Tex-Mex – are Chinga. Deros. They look like any normal little ant, like you might have way up north, the ones that show up and ruin your picnic, or find that spilled sugar or piece of candy or food you may have dropped under the sofa.

But they don't just show up and take food, hoisting the pieces of fried chicken over their heads and marching off into the ant-hill nearby, never to bother you again.

Most of the time a Fire Ant mound* can be spotted in time to avoid it, especially after it rains. The newly mined dark soil can be seen rising up through the Zoisia grass pretty easily, all flaky and inviting like a fresh-baked chocolate cake with a bit much baking powder in

---

*"Hills" are for normal, respectful ants.

it. But if your grass is too long, or if the cake didn't rise high enough, you will step into the soft, giving earth, and immediately regret your life choices.

DO NOT try to shake them off your foot. Just take off your boots, douse them in gasoline and set them on fire. They are dead to you now.

You may need to burn your pants, as well.

And while you are at it, just soak your yard with gas and light it up. If your house catches the burn, so be it: there are fire ants in it also.

Any ants that make it to your skin will bite.

They bite, they bite hard, and they don't like to let go. The bite stings like some sort of very stingy thing. Or may also feel like, I don't know, fire or something.

And they don't bite only when agitated, no. Unlike so many members of the Animal Kingdom that only bite when provoked (dogs, snakes, spiders, etc.), as soon as Fire Ants touch your skin, the godless little monsters' mandibles sink in like you have slapped them twice and called them Aggies.

Seconds later you feel the burn. The pain could possibly go unnoticed for a second or two, so that by the time you DO notice, the poison has worked itself in good. Later on the itch sets in, which you WILL scratch. Scratching might alleviate the pain for a few seconds, but it always comes back with a vengeance.

If the ant had enough time to pump adequate venom into your flesh, you will get a pimple afterward. A big ol' white-headed pimple, as the white blood cells rush to administer first aid and fight the venom. When you pop this pimple, as you are definitely going to want to do (because who doesn't love popping pimples?), and drain it... it will itch even more, and it will take forever to heal. It will scab over, then you'll scratch it, it will flake off, then eventually in a few weeks-to-months all you'll be lucky to have is a very faint red mark to remind you.

If you're unlucky, you'll look like a confused/ADHD heroine addict with poor aim... dark red spots all over your body.

By the way, you almost never get bitten by just one, lone fire ant. If you disturb a nest with your hands or feet, by the time you see the swarm of activity as they rush to repair and reconstruct their hive, and perhaps adjust their eggs that were close to the surface, you've already got three dozen on you somewhere. The good news? In a few seconds you'll know exactly where they all are.

The reason I bring up Fire Ants at all is this: Fire Ants are like poorly-thought-out decisions in life.

There are wrong choices everywhere, and by the time you've noticed a few of them, you're already too late, as the repercussions will soon make themselves known. And the itch from those wrong choices? It will bug you for quite some time on average, even if it's just remembering that stupid thing you did or said a mere 24 years ago, and got immediate karma from it.

The memory will be bad enough to make you cringe again – PHYSICALLY CRINGE – just by thinking about it. That's not even a metaphor.

I have a couple dozen memories in my head of stupid shit I have done or said dating back as far as Middle School, that make me *actually flinch* when I think of them.

If only Poor Life Choices were as easy to see as fresh-built Fire Ant mounds.

Sometimes a Poor Life Choice looks like a bong being passed around in a group of relative unknowns, sometimes it looks like a leaky toilet tank that you are certain you can fix in a jiff. Sometimes it looks like a really hot man or woman you see across the bar after a few too many Jager Bombs.

Perhaps poor choices look like you, 30 years ago, in your prime, when you could have easily done that thing that you just did, but you are actually 55 now – and the years have not been so kind to your physique – so for the rest of your life, you will sound like a car trying to start on a cold morning whenever you bend over to pick up anything you dropped on the floor. That floor will feel very far away, and ultimately, you should leave the thing there that you dropped, and start your new life without it.

We've all made a few bad choices in our lives, amiright? If you're over a certain age, I'll just bet you have. (If you haven't, you need to make some before it is too late.) If you need to know if it is a poor life choice, it's pretty easy to tell. In your mind, a little voice in the back of your head will say something akin to this:

"This is going to leave a mark."

or

"I REALLY should not be doing this."

or

"I am SOOO gonna get boned on this, aren't I?"

But the hallmark of a Poor Life Choice, is that despite hearing from that little voice inside your head, or from the actual mouth of a real-live person standing next to you, a Poor Life Choice is always the chosen one regardless of the admonishments against choosing it.

"I'm going to take the wheels off my teacher's chair, so she'll look funny trying to get it to roll," may sound good in your head when you're eleven, but surprise: it is not a good life choice. It will definitely buy you a trip to the principal's office.

You know this, you do it anyway.

Or perhaps, when you are 16, and working at an amusement park in high school, you and a friend want to impress a couple girls who work in the Controller's Office, where all the money from the park is deposited at the end of the day. So you choose to play a funny prank, where you wait in line to get in, and as soon as the door is buzzed for you to enter, you pull out your 110 instamatic camera case, and your friend pulls his sunglasses case, and you pretend to "hold up the bank." "It'll be hilarious," you think to yourself, "especially if the two security guards don't go for their guns and shoot us both dead." With an emphasis on hoping the two security guards don't pull their guns and shoot you both dead.* I know it feels VERY counter intuitive, but this is also a

---

*This particular thing is a really REALLY bad idea. Do not EVER do this.

marginally Poor Life Choice. Even if half the people in that room know who you are.

You know this, you do it anyway.

"Hey, what do you think about a third..." you start to ask your wife a few years later, interrupted by an out-of-nowhere, highly accurate and oddly curated slap across your face that you just know is going to leave a welt.

"No, wait, I was only going to say, what would you think about having a third chi..." SAAAAAA-LAPPPPP. There goes a small piece of your face skin that stuck to the palm of your wife's hand.

Okay... a gimmee there on that one – VERY Poor Life Choice. Circle that one in red. Underline it. Do NOT do it anyway.

Poor Life Choices can be made at any age or stage of life; but making them when you are younger is advised, so that you learn from them by the time you are older. Unless you're dumb, or pig-headed, or perhaps both.

Case in point.

You are in the latter half of your fifth decade of life, plus you own a Large Thing. In fact, let's be more precise and call it what it is: a Large, Heavy Thing. And this Large, Heavy Thing has been sitting where is for years, not *really* bothering anyone at all.

But the more you look at this Large, Heavy Thing, the less you can stand the damned sight of it and how it just... *be's there*... for years.

"Someday, I'm gonna move that Large, Heavy Thing

to the upstairs, where I won't have to look at it anymore," you thinks to yourself.

"No," says your wife, trying to be all voice-of-reason and shit. "Just leave it, you are not 25 anymore, we'll get someone to move it."

Smash Zoom in to your open-mouthed facial reaction:

"Did my own wife just diss me?" you think to yourself. Rightfully so, I might add.

You are still young and virile, and that Large, Heavy Thing wasn't so heavy when you moved it in there at age 29. And it's only been maybe 6, 8, what, 25 years since it came to set on that spot. The HELL does she mean, *"you're only trying to move it because you're afraid to choose the option of getting someone else to do it, because that would mean admitting how old and out of shape you are?"*

"Me?" you sputter like a Proper English Gentleman who has just been told he isn't allowed to colonize any more countries, "Afraid? ME? When I had the carpal tunnel syndrome, did I not choose to get both hands operated on at the same time... on Friday the 13th... during Covid?

"I'm not afraid of hard choices. I got huge chunks of hard choices in my morning stool." You bluster.

So, as soon as your significant other is out of the house for a reasonable amount of time (VERY important, as if they are not home, they can not stop you), you CHOOSE to get the dolly, strap the Large, Heavy Thing onto the dolly, and muscle that 250-pound atrocity-against-nature up that set of stairs, pop it over that bullnose top step you thought looked like nothing until the tiny tires of the uber-laden dolly had to get over it.

You are all-in now, so you make one last mighty (chosen) HEAVE to get it around that tight corner and into the room.

Then you (handpick the idea to) collapse onto the carpet like ANY man would, young or old(er); (resolving to) huff and pant like an asthmatic Death Valley hill sprinter as you try not to (decide to) pass out from the lack of oxygen to your muscles. The amount of O2 to your brain has not diminished one iota, you can think clearly the whole time you lie there, staring at the ceiling.

Twenty or thirty virile minutes later – when you are good and ready to do so, you (may wish to) stand up again – so you do so. Slowly (out of choice). Only a chicken-shit would stand right up in two seconds, anyway. You take all the time you want, you've earned it, by GOD. And, secure enough in your manhood as you are, you (opt to) put a hand on your lower back as you waddle to the wall for support.

See? Who's afraid to ask for help, now, Life Partner? You lean on that wall all you want to, 'tis a free country, buddy, nobody is going to think any less of you. And if you (have a hankering to) yelp a tiny little yip of excruciating pain, it is your CONSTITUTIONAL RIGHT to do so.

By the way, the manner in which you make it over to the top of the stairs again... well some of the toughest hombres in the world (adopt the notion to) walk that way.

John Wayne, Walter Brennan, Julius Caesar. You're in good company.

You may (preselect the whim to) hold that bannister with both hands as you physically stutter down those stairs one every minute-and-a-half, you've got NOTHING to prove by walking normally. Give in to the caprice of finding your balance again on each step as you go. Ain't NOBODY demanding taking away your (dibs on) walking like a drunken new-born giraffe.

"Not 25 anymore," my ASS. Would a 25-year-old grab a beer and wash down three Tylenol and a handful of ibuprofen and then eeeeeeeaaaaaase onto the couch and (elect to) not be able to get comfortable for like ten whole minutes? I doubt it. I know for DANG sure some young stud wouldn't be man enough to drive himself to the Minute Clinic down the road and get an Xray of his lower spine – just as a (personally prerogatived) preventative measure. Wouldn't want a crushed vertebra slappin' on the ol' spinal cord when you go to pull the engine out of your car this weekend.

A younger man would never (settle upon the conviction to) cry out in pain before the doctor has even touched their back because they knew what was coming. Thatta GROWN ASSED MAN thang. Pain Pills? Muscle relaxers? HEEEEEELLLs yeah, my ego is not so inflated that I'm ashamed to ask for the maximum dosage. Call that shit in to My Boy at the Walgreens on 183.

TOO OLD? BIIIIIISH, more like TWO WORDS: Puh and Leaze.

As the pain killers, anti-inflammatories, and muscle

relaxants start to kick in, the feeling starts to slowly synapse-hop back into your lower spine, kinda feeling like a small swarm of fire ants piercing the flesh around your L1 to L5. Hell, you may have even created an L6 and 7 for your effort.

"Ahhhh," you sigh, "that went just how I knew it would. You still got it, Greg. Good choice..."

BRING
OUT
YOUR
DEAD

I have seen a few dead bodies in my lifetime, but have never seen a person actually die before. I mean, if you take away that time when I was very young, and the first recorded images of the Vietnam War were being broadcast on TV. Soldiers were advancing on some building, there was gunfire, and one of those soldiers fell, and then they cut away to something else quite quickly. That soldier could have lived, maybe he just went prone to be a smaller target. Who knows. It was weird to see on TV, what with not being a movie and all, and I'm not quite sure I understood what was happening, anyway.

But that's all beside the point.

So, dead people. The first real live dead human bodies I remember seeing were when I was in high school, during a field trip in Anatomy & Physiology class. Mr. Moore got us all on a bus and we headed for the Virginia Medical College in Richmond, where we were to observe actual cadavers in a lab setting.

Like most of the other students in class, I'm pretty sure I had little practical idea of what to expect in a medical-grade dead body, and even less idea of how to compose myself in such a setting. I mean, wiggling a subscapularis muscle from a cat in my lab partner Carol's face in Anatomy, or secretly attaching the sticky rear legs of a dozen grasshoppers to the back of Ms. Langmeade's sweater every time she passed our table in Biology II, were one thing. Sitting in on a bunch of medical students slicing up real dead *human* bodies was another. I knew *that*, at least.

The bus ride to the Medical College was pretty uneventful, unless you count the giant, lumbering basketball-playing classmate who shot daggers from his eyes at me because I got the last available bench seat in the bus, and he had to sit in the stairwell next to Mr. Moore.

Why the hell did he single me out anyway, there were two dozen other kids who got on that bus together. Why was I the only uncaring bastard who wouldn't give up a seat for him. I mean Jesus, there was way more room in the freakin' stairwell anyway. Okay, I clearly had to watch my back with that guy around the scalpels and bone saws.

The Medical College was pretty impressive, I have to admit. Even allowing that the technology of 1981

Virginia was probably as to today's equipment and techniques as Mary Shelley's time was to 1981 Virginia... it was still sooooo Sciency.

The lab tables were these stainless steel vats, like sarcophaguses, or perhaps metal Tupperware containers, filled with formaldehyde. The bodies were in a sort of deep-fryer basket that sat down in the preservation liquid. The basket was lifted, the goo drained out, and the body was set on the work surface using medical grade BBQ tongs.

It was the smell that hit you like a brick upon first entering the room.

These students were already well into the whatever-week's-worth of the cadaver study, their allotted bodies in different stages of cut-upness and decay, so that even with the magic juice, there was a notable aroma.

Oh, but my gosh, arms removed, chest cavities laid open, heads sawn in twain... it was fantastic. One student was on his way to disconnecting a pacemaker from the chest of an older man's body. Another was removing and weighing a brain, and still another was working on the vascular system of the right arm of her person. The un-working brachial artery was like a garden hose.

We asked about where the bodies came from, and were informed that these study aids were "left to Science," meaning that the people who once inhabited them, stated that they wanted their empty conveyances to be used for educational purposes after they passed. Well, that was a pretty interesting service, and mighty selfless of them folks to allow it.

What a learning experience. Unforgettable. For me, at least; I cannot speak for my classmates. Though I will go out on a severed limb here and say that anyone seeing a dead *human* body for the first time will remember it for quite some time, possibly in vivid detail. It does capture one's attention.

That is why I urge everyone to think very hard on the subject of having an open casket wake or viewing for loved ones, especially when younger folks might be included in viewing the remains. I know, it can be a learning experience, and young people *do* need to learn about death eventually. I guess I am of two minds about the whole thing.

The reason I ask you think about it, is because this not-alive image can remain in the mind of the viewer, and you might not want *that* version of the deceased to be all that is remembered from there on out.

My paternal grandmother died youngish, she was 76. She got cancer, which did not do wonders for her diabetes and complications thereof. It started in her stomach, spread to her head and then everywhere else; it took a while to take her down. In fact, the formal COD was "pneumonia." This formality on death certificates kind of bothers me; just writing down the extremely specific actuality, and not really saying what led up to it. No mention of the fact that her body was worn the hell out from the meds she was taking to help with the cancer in her diabetes-weakened body, and that condition messed with her so much that she got pneumonia, and THAT'S what finished her off.

I mean, yeah, *technically*, she could have beaten the cancer were it not for the pneumonia, but hell, even in hockey the players who assist the goal-maker get credit.

I stayed in the hospital with her the weekend before she passed away, my grandfather had been by her side for a long time, and he was pretty tired, so he went home to get cleaned up and get some real sleep. I slept in a chair by her bed, was given a quick tutorial in how the wall suction worked so I could help clear out her throat if needed. None of *that* really bothered me too much.

What *did* bother me was realizing that Grandma's mind was still quite sharp.

We talked a lot that last weekend, and as bad as she was, I could still make her laugh on occasion. I found an oldies TV channel and I remember watching Laurel and Hardy one night, about 2 am. They were singing and dancing to "Shine On Harvest Moon," and Grandma was telling me how much she and Grandpa loved them back in the day.

While talking with her, it occurred to me how much it had to suck to watch yourself waste away, and know what was coming next. From then on, I hoped to get hit by a bus when I had my head turned. As grumpy and cranky as my grandmother was, I didn't think anyone should have to see it coming from a mile away, especially not while still incredibly lucid.

Yeah, Grandma was cranky for most of the time I knew her, and I am sure she had her reasons why, but cranky nonetheless. So when, at the Viewing, I looked down into the casket and saw this forced grimace on her face, I simply saw Grandma. It tracked, spot-on; nice job Funeral Home Face Adjustment Guy. Very natural. I would gladly tip 20%.

A few years later, upon hearing of my grandfather's (her husband's) death, I had to fly back to New York for the funeral. Mind you, we had just moved to Texas way less than a year before he passed. I had a dreaded feeling he was going to go when I wasn't there, and that sort of bugged me. I was really pissed when my dad called to tell me the news. *I just knew it.*

Being in the life-place we were in – a brand new baby, and a five-year-old, and new to this city/state – we were not rolling in money. We had to be clever about travel, especially up to that part of the country where it was not a direct flight. Then you'd also have to rent a car in Albany, or Burlington, or Montreal, and drive a few hours.

I flew to Albany: cheaper, better choice of arrival hours. Somehow, without the magic of cell phones, I managed to coordinate with my brother to meet at the airport and drive up together. Even with the planning, my plane was delayed for weather and I got in way late.

We called the funeral home to see if we could still make it up there to view the body, as the burial was the next morning.

The director said he'd hold it ("It" being our grandfather) until we got there, which turned out to be pretty late, after 9pm I think. We were the only ones there. I rushed in, walked right up the casket, looked down, and reflexively jerked my head back with a confused look on my face.

Who the hell was that in Grandpa's box? THAT'S not my grandfather.

I mean, it *kinda* looked like him... but he had the same sour look on his face that my grandmother had. That "WHAT? Are you *kidding* me? I'M DEAD? SERIOUSLY? I am NOT diggin' this," look. This might have been fine for Grandma – she always looked that way – but seeing that same look on my generally happy-go-lucky grandfather just looked waaaaaaaayyy out of place.

And then it dawned on me – holy cow, Funeral Home Face Adjustment Guy had a *very* limited bag of tricks to work with. *This* was his Go-To expression. Pretty much *everybody* he works on just winds up with this horrid thousand-yard stare. I mean, the eyes being open would DEFINITELY have been *much* creepier, but you get me. Not cool; not cool AT ALL.

What a rip.

You're a happy, fun person your whole life, and in the end you just look like a sour old Russian woman who had to cook pot-after-pot of kielbasa and sauerkraut year-after-year? THAT seemed highly disrespectful, and felt almost bait-and-switchy on the funeral home's part. THAT'S going on Yelp, for DAMN sure.

Every subsequent viewing or wake I attended after that, I made sure to check the faces of the departed for any signs of personality that was not "I am a corpse, and I do NOT approve of this," and I have been sorely disappointed at *every last one*.

I was actually worried for years that I would only remember Grandpa as that gloomy, grimacing ghoul in a suit. Thankfully, I eventually lost the image of that Last Look, and now only remember the wide smile with the gap between his teeth, the bushy eyebrows and that twinkly look in his eyes again.

So... open box, or framed photo on the lid, it's up to you. Don't feel bad if you miss the wake, although sometimes they do the job. I know at my grandmother's viewing, we all sat around having a pretty good time with the memories, laughing quite a bit, catching up with relatives who we didn't see very often.

I got to see one of my cousins that I had not seen in quite some time, she and I probably laughed way more than was appropriate for the situation. Even my grandma's sister, who was always a lot of fun, laughed between the tears.

I felt a bit cheated years later when *they* both passed away. I was unable to attend my Great Aunt's funeral, did not have the wherewithal to get back to Yonkers for it. I felt bad about that. But I knew she was happy now. She waited a long time to get there; she wanted to be reunited with her husband who had died decades before.

When my cousin passed away, as with her father who went about six months before her, there was no wake, no funeral for family and friends – at least that is what I was told. No request for flowers or donations, I couldn't even find obituaries for them in the papers or online. I guess they had the mentality that you're here for a certain amount of time, you live your life, then you pass from this world... and there ain't no fanfare, life goes on. And in a way, I can get behind that.

I totally understand the sentiment of the "Life Goes On" and we are "All Just Cogs in a Machine." Especially when it comes to how much the Funeral Business gouges out of Grief's wallet. And it galls me no end that Funeral Home Face Adjustment Guy gets paid anything at all. He should work for tips only. THAT would help bump up his game, I bet.

But funerals are not for the dead: they're for the living. Personally I *would* have liked to have said goodbye to my Great Aunt, and Uncle, and Cousin – but I didn't *really* need a ceremony and special building. I could have – and did – do that from wherever I was at the time. Though I will also admit that it's easier to focus on the box, I suppose. There is a real closure to be had from the closure of that box.

Whatever the situation post-mortem, whether it be a stainless steel sarcophagus and bone saws, or some unrecognizable face pulled up into a smile (?), I wouldn't worry too much about it. The human mind being what it is, you will wind up having the good memories of the person you'll have, well after all that temporal hoopla and novelty of death passes away.

FOOD
FOR
THOUGHT

Sometimes I overthink things, *according to my wife*. To me, though, I am not really over-thinking things, but rather giving the *proper amount* of thought to things that most people do not think about enough. Or think about in *that way*. But either which, it is the correct amount of thought, and I should be credited with having the fortitude to decide to think about the things that others will not.

Such as: so far, I have not managed to kill any family member with my cooking.

I know on the surface this sounds like I am being self-effacing, making it look like I *don't really care* that my attempts at familicide have all failed, and all I have ended up doing for over 40 years is just feeding people who are related to me. But really, I am just noting that I can, and have indeed, cooked and baked for many years, and fed that food to people who were – quite frankly – under no real obligation to either consume or enjoy what I served them. And none of them have died from it. Yet.

Facts.

Information.

Faces have been made. Items have been hidden under napkins. Portions have been slipped to pets. Every goll-danged meal has always been either too much or too little. The different elements of the plating were all touching each other, and goddamnit, why were there *onions* in this?

But NO ONE – meaning "not one person" – has died from eating what I have made for either breakfast, lunch, or dinner. Or any snack or dessert in-between. Now, I am in no way bragging about my kitchen prowess; I know I am a pretty functional cook at absolute best.

That is, I can cook food, but am by no means a professional. I did not ask my kids to shout "YES, CHEF!" when they added the chocolate chips to the cookie batter when prompted to stop shoving them one by one into their own cake holes. I did not wear a jaunty white, poofy Chef's hat when cooking... almost EVER.* And though I never bragged about my ability or any particular dish I made, I always knew that I could cook

---

*There is a picture out there somewhere, of me at age five or so, wearing a white poofy Chef's hat as I "helped" my father or mother bake something. I did not ask for it, nor did I know the significance of it. My dad would frequently wear one when cooking, barbecuing, or even when making Maple Syrup.

just fine, and if we had food lying around at dinner time, I could likely make something to eat.

I only mention this because I have watched a lot of cooking shows where the chef was making something pretty complicated, and they whizzed right through it like it was *nothing*. All the folks whose job it was to sample the food at the end, made "ooh and ahhh" sounds come out of their stuffed faces and said how great it was. I sat there with my eyebrows knit up, wondering at the spectacle of it all. How could anyone have the ability to just zip through some fancy recipe, or just sort of "wing it" to come up with this fantastic dish everyone loved.

"Oh wow," tasters would say, "the caramelized onions just melt in your mouth."

Or

"Sacre Bleu, these amalgamized beef medallions have actually bonded over trust exercises with the drizzle of truffle enhancement."

Or

"NEVER in my LIFE have I eaten ANYTHING as exquisite as this! The reconstituted macerated cardamom constructs pair iconically with the pejorative nut meat assumptions, creating a strobe of flavor and texture that lambasts my mouth with invocations of tastebudical tumultuousness."

I have, on occasion, gotten "this is really good Dad," or "OH BOY! Tacos!"

But I have never gotten any of those other well-thought-out exclamations of embarrassing pedantic praise from my family, and certainly not anything even close from total strangers.

In fact, on the rare occasions when I was tasked with cooking for others, it has ended quite tragically. And this is where I have learned that doing anything under that sort of pressure does not work out well for me. It is anxiety-inducing, and stymies me no end.

I have made maybe 37 Thanksgiving meals for family over the years. Most of them objectively good, many of them downright tasty, and all of them edible. All of them 90 to 100% from scratch, and dang near every gosh-darn one without a written recipe.

Conversely, I have made two dinners for friends that had come over to share the holiday with us... and I felt like a chimp whose stick kept breaking when trying to get ants out of a log to impress a hungry, would-be mate.

Turkey was dry, stuffing was tasteless, cranberry sauce* was too tart and overly-jellied, and worst of all, the pies. Flat, burned... basically frisbees with a fruit filling, or pumpkin with a consistency that could easily hold together the stonework in the garden. What an utter foodical disaster.

The only thing that could possibly have made things worse would be if the friend that had come over had brought his family with him, and they were all rather posh and full of themselves to begin with.

---

*Which I proudly make by hand from scratch every year. It is eaten only by me, because my entire family is a bunch of low-brow jerks who only eat the canned crap.

Yeah. That. Happened.

What an *oddly specific* curse to have to suffer through life with. Who on Earth did my ancestors piss off, *in what way*, to be cursed with *only being able to cook if it is for myself or my immediate family*?

It happens with drinks too. I can mix drinks if it's just us; have you tried my Sangria? I can make a pretty dang decent mojito as well. *But bring over friends*? Suddenly I can't muddle mint in a glass any better than I could muddle a wet cat into a blender with a slinky.

Mortifying.

The only saving grace is that most of the family and friends are pretty forgiving about it. There are respectful smiles and nods all around to my face... to make up for the scraping and pouring of foodstuffs and drinks into our indoor potted plants and sofa cushions.

Me, most of the time, as I have written before, am not a picky eater or drinker at all. Any time there is food to eat, and drink to drink – and I didn't have to make it – I'm a pretty happy camper. That being said, I do not like the sauce known as Mole (pronounced Mole) at all. Especially not the ones containing chocolate, which, from what little I know, is most of them.

Yet once, a good friend of my wife invited us over for lunch; his mother was heading back home to Mexico, so she wanted to cook him a good-bye meal for his friends. Mole was on the menu. My wife, knowing my secret dislikature, shot me a glance when the meal was brought out by this tiny little 70-year-old-woman who looked like she would collapse under the weight of epicurean shame if someone did not like her cooking.

She brought out the plated food, and lovingly smiled as she doused it all with mole shot from a high-pressure firehose before I could politely scream "Dear God, NO!"

I have very little social skill, so I did not know what the proper etiquette was for backing away from food like it was a deranged chimp with a hand grenade; I just ate it, thinking I was a good enough actor to pull it off. This version of the sauce was actually pretty good, so that helped a LOT.

Mind you, I am wholly on-board with trying almost anything at least once. Bat, scorpion, or almost anything fried on a stick; guinea pig, horse or any non-traditional food animal; insects, grubs right out of the ground; even artisanal home-brewed craft IPA from an Austin hipster food truck. I have had plenty of opportunities for some type of food or drink to pick a fight with my taste-buds or stomach functions.

Hence, I am proud to say that I can pretty much count on not all the fingers of one hand the times in my life that I just flat-out *could not* eat something that was served to me. And I mean I could not even stand the *thought* of putting the food into my mouth, nearly retching at the mere idea. And two of those three times... were my own cooking.

The very first time was years ago. My parents were still married so I had to be under the age of ten; pretty sure I was maybe 6 or so. My mom made these meatballs – not the normal, trusted, good-ol' homemade puhsketticompliment type meatwads – but fancy-schmancy nonsense from some bullshit 1970s transcendental cookbook. Not Swedish ones, I am pretty sure. These had this *smell* – I refuse to even call it an aroma – of a rancid, decaying animal in an alley or something.

I could barely get one to my mouth before my gag reflex kicked in. And we all know what young children are like when it comes to hiding their feelings for the benefit of someone else. Of course we all know *me* by now as well. The disapproval was NOT getting quashed.

What really got me was that nobody else seemed to have the same reaction. Why were they eating these disgusting globs of yech and NOT barfing?

"How do you like them, honey?" my mom asked, clearly understanding that I hated them with every fiber of my being.

I could not answer, because opening my mouth would undo all the good I had accomplished by pinching my nose shut and puffing out my cheeks. So I just shook my head a tiny bit and said nothing.

Shit. *That* caught Dad's attention. You shouldn't move near my father. For if he saw you move, he'd know where you were. And if you were in arm's reach, well, you might as well swallow the cyanide capsule on the end of your fork before his beefy hand found that tender spot above and below your clavicle that allowed him to use your collar bone as a handle with which to lift and toss you like a giant Curling Stone.

"Eat it, or go to bed without any sup..." he started.

I was racing up the stairs before the sentence finished leaving his mouth, pumping my fist in celebration that this was the worst I got, and considering myself lucky to have dodged two bullets and all it cost was going to bed hungry. I could recoup my nutritional losses in the morning with an extra giant bowl of cereal if I woke up before my older brother.

The second and third times I was unable to eat – or even entertain the thought of eating – something that was put in front of me, was much later in my life. I was married and had kids already, and had spent some time being rather creative with my cooking. But what got me the second time was some white fish I made. I want to say it was Orange Roughy, which we ate all the time.

And oddly enough, once again, nobody else *had the same reaction*. I took one bite, and could not swallow it; it was thence surreptitiously hocked into my napkin like a mother bird feeding her young. I looked around the table at the other five folks eating away, wondering if they would drop one by one, starting very soon. But no. They happily ate away. My wife looked at me, eyes darting from my plate to my face a few times.

"What's the matter?" she asked quietly.

"How does it taste to you?" I answered, not expecting to understand her words, because surely her tongue had swollen to five times its normal size from the poisoned poisson.

"It's very good," she said – and this is the part that killed me – in a rather sincere and genuine tone.

I picked at the veggies and rice, found them to be

palatable, and scarfed them up. Leaving the offending fillet to return to the dust from whence it came right there on my plate.

"Anybody else... uhhhh, not like the fish?" I queried, hoping someone would validate me; how could I possibly be the *only one*?

Nobody.

They all thought it was anywhere from "just fine," to "pretty good." I shook my head, and just sat out the rest of the meal like a Vegan in a barbeque joint. Our daughter doesn't even *like* white fish, and she ate it all.

Those were the worst of the three, quite frankly I cannot even recall what the third one was, but it was a similar situation. And I was just as baffled.

It's the sort of thing that gets one thinking. Thinking of things like how old I was, and how many meals I had to have eaten in that time; and how many of those meals were cooked by me myself. And what were the chances, out of say a sample of 100 meals, that not even ONE would be something I couldn't eat?

You know, like 7 out of a hundred, or maybe 10% sounded pretty practical and reasonable to me; taking into consideration eating places you never knew anything about before, or some restaurant having a bad day, or a girlfriend/boyfriend trying to impress you with a vegetarian lasagna that fell quite short.

I'm pretty much 60 years old now; so, for the sake of easy math, let's just use the typical breakfast-lunch-dinner triptych of meals to average out – making up for skipped meals, two years of wrestling, overeating in the good years, a few years of not having any money for food in college or the first years of marriage, etc. That makes 65,700 meals eaten... with only three – THREE – that I could not physically eat.

Do I have an eating disorder? Am I unable to discern foods/flavors? Does my mind not register awfulness or yuck-factor? Do I have a mutant ability to not die when food-poisoned? Am I living in a simulation, or maybe I was already dead, and this was my personalized version of Hell?

Aliens? Was it Aliens? I'll bet it was Aliens.

This is the type of shit that actually went through my mind as I sat there the two times as an adult when I could not eat my own cooking.

My wife, kids and, when-present, in-laws, probably thought I was having a stroke, just sitting there with a blank look on my face and un-touched food on my plate. They knew that normally I eat every last crumb in front of me, so this was noteworthy, and undoubtedly a little frightening for them.

"What's the matter with Dad?" our son asked, as he separated all the different elements of food and arranged them on his plate so they didn't touch each other, and he could then eat them from a north-west to south-east order.

"Are his eyes glazing over?" our daughter said, as she hoped no one noticed her scraping her green beans into the aquarium just behind her as they all looked at my Buster Keaton-styled face.

"Oh my goodness," my mother-in-law almost whispered, in that far-away, matter-of-factish voice that someone gets when they clearly don't care.

"Give me his plate," chimed in my father-in-law.

But my wife knew. We'd been married long enough. She reached over, took my hand gently in hers and said

"You're trying to figure out 'Why' aren't you?"

Yeah, I was.

And still am.

QUESTIONABLE AUTHORITY

A lot of folks over the years have told me I have a big problem with authority, and/or authority figures. But what do those dumbasses know.

I do *not*. What I *do* have is a problem with:

- People who set themselves up as authorities with nothing more than threats, ultimatums, or the statement "Because I said so"

- Those who say that they have all the answers, and everyone else is wrong and usually stupid

- Individuals who say they are "only Playing Devil's Advocate," but in reality they just want to psyche you out or impose their beliefs on you

- Folks that talk a good game, but their actions do not match what they say at all

Those people... I have a *huge* problem with.

The fact that these behaviors tend to show up a lot on folks with some level of authority is not something I can control. I do not recognize *their* authority, and I do not like to be shoved into compliance with them or anyone else who tells me to just "go with the flow," and "welp, they are in charge, soooo..."

That really grinds my pepper.

Authority figures should not rule by fear, bragging, misdirection, or trying to control the narrative; they should have authority because of knowledge, experience and respect that is earned, not force-fed. And they should not abuse the position and power that is theirs. I don't think this is an unreasonable request or expectation. If it is, I will certainly take the hit, but it feels like the absolute LEAST One can do and still be an authority figure that others would believe in and follow.

I know I don't have a problem with *just anyone* who is in charge, because I have had plenty of work – and personal – relationships that I enjoyed quite a bit where the "Bosses" were from a wide range of demographics. But I also learned to know the difference between when someone was genuinely interested in leading, and when they just wanted to take advantage of "being in charge."

Someone *actually* trying to play Devil's Advocate – presumably to help you think through a decision you were about to make, ensuring you thought of everything – asks questions and talks *to* you. Those that talk *at* you, or *down* to you, are a different thing.

They are called assholes.

Now, just because I do not particularly care for these types of people does not in any way mean I know how to handle them, to this very day. But I do get a certain kick out of being right and showing what the Emperor is wearing on occasion; and I do sometimes love it when I'm right – even at a steep cost.

Nothing made me chuckle to myself more than showing this particular person was a tool bag when he had been going around work making friends with everybody, and acting like the hip New Kid on the Block one year.

He strolled in from out of town (he was 'an old friend' of the Boss), was put in a high place of power within the office, and immediately started ingratiating himself. My-oh-MY, he could just be Mr. Friendly-Pants; he knew how to tell a joke, and it was just *soooo* easy to talk to him. Just perfect. *Too perfect.*

I was suspicious right away.

To me, anyone who is *too* perfect, I just don't trust. *Always* fun and in a good mood, knows just what to say, *never* loses their composure, or talks too much about themselves, etc. Even the most caring, fun, and helpful folks out there have bad days and off moments, we're Human. This guy never had an "off" day or moment.

NOBODY is 100% ANYTHING. This guy had clearly taken a weekend seminar in how to win people over, he probably earned double gold in Throw-Back-Your-Head-To-Laugh-At-Anything-Even-Remotely-

Funny-That-Others-Say. He had a hidden agenda that *required* this facade. Mostly... it was his *eyes*. He just had mean, lying eyes.

I first met him at an office Christmas Party, a friend came up and said,

"Oh, here's that guy I've been telling you about! You got to meet him!"

I did. We chatted a few minutes, he was very funny. And laid back. And VERY interested in me and what I had to say about my coworkers and job. After a few minutes, Friendly-Pants walked away to chat up someone else, excusing himself after giving me a so-very-slight look up and down. When he was out of hearing range, I turned to my friend and said flatly

"He's here to fire people."

My friend just looked at me like I said I'd like to kill and eat his dog it in front of him.

"What the hell are you talking about?" he asked with almost a hurt look on his face.

"He asked a lot of questions about you, and me, and the others in our department," I said, "every time I asked him about himself, he expertly avoided answering anything. He wasn't having friendly party conversation, he was grabbing intel."

Well, my friend must have said something to him eventually, because the next couple of times we went out for drinks over the next few weeks, Friendly-Pants made some very overt, albeit vague attempts to "open up" about himself.

My friend said something like

"See, he talks about himself. He's okay."

One of the great tricks I have picked up by being an actor, is being able to spot some Grade-A Horseshit from a mile away.

"Really. Tell me something you just learned about him that was specific," I asked.

My friend couldn't. He just repeated some of the vague Mind-Reader Talk-to-the-Spirits kind of shit you see Carnival Hucksters do when trying to hook a crowd. My friend made a face, looked down, looked back toward Friendly-Pants, and shut up.

Then another week or so in, people started to lose their jobs. Seems *somebody* knew all kinds of shit that would never have been known if someone hadn't talked; or if someone hadn't talked within earshot of *someone else* who was "just being friendly." Departments lost heads, and then somehow those departments now moved under the auspices of Mr. You-Know-Whomst.

And GOD DAMN, if people didn't STILL believe his line of garbage.

Then one day at lunch, a bunch of us were sitting around eating and Friendly-Pants walks up and sits and just starts chatting like he's everybody's buddy, makes a crack or two about me, then really focuses on me, trying to get everyone to turn on me. I didn't mind much, I wasn't going to be there that much longer anyway, my four-year stretch was coming to an end.

So I found a chink or two in his armor, and just dug

in, and I would not let it go. *Thank you Mother's-Side-Grandpa, for that personality trait.* I talked to my friends as normal, but kept referring to Friendly-Pants as "The Cool Kid."

Finally he got really frustrated that he wasn't getting anywhere... and I guess his new nick-name wasn't sitting well with him. He slammed his hands on the table and stood up,

"I don't have to put up with this shit," he declared. "Who do you think you are? (Ironically a question I had internally been asking him for months)" he spat.

I just smiled at him.

"I win." I stated.

He was red-faced furious, and stormed away.

The firings got more brutal, long-time good employees were let go unceremoniously, and Friendly-Pants's power grew exponentially. Anybody who was not on board was kicked to the curb.

They found out later that he did this for living. He was hired to come in, root out those who were not 100% bought-in on the company and the way the CEO did things – by way of insinuating himself into the various groups and cliques and mining information. And then he culled the herd.

He had his sights set on being CEO when the current Turd-In-Residence retired. He thought he had found a forever home. So I laughed pretty hard when he was finally passed over for a C-Line position, because nobody could stand him anymore, and that feeling bled into the Board of Directors.

I'm happy people finally saw him for what he was, but not happy about the way it happened. I like to think folks got an idea what he was about in time to head off some real damage, but I guess one way or the other it was happening anyway. Pretty disgusting when people treat others like shit just for their own ego-feeding or to save a buck.

I wasn't always that good at reading folks though, and I knew even less about how to handle those sorts of people and situations when I was a kid. In my teens, it would have saved me a lot of emotional scarring and beating up on myself. I always had to learn the very hard way. Because I just wasn't quick enough on my feet, and doubted myself all the time; and worse yet, if somebody was "In Charge" I tended to think there was a good reason for it and I never questioned it much.

In High School, when I started wrestling, I was, as usual, late to the party. Especially in rural Virginia, where kids started wrestling at age two, and by the time they were 10 already had trophies covering a wall in their bedroom, if not also some state medal hanging from their car's rear-view mirror.

Me? I started at age 15 from scratch.

I had a friend that wrestled, he was wiry, an inch or so taller than me. We hung out a lot, we had a lot in common. One day in Biology class he asked me if I ever wrestled, I said no, just chickens and turkeys and the occasional pig. Why?

"You're built like a wrestler," he said, "low center of gravity – I bet you'd be good at it."

I had never really thought about it, but I guess my formative years on a farm did do something for me physically. And the summer between 9th and 10th grades, I grew pretty big; not taller, but wider.

"Really?" I asked, genuinely surprised, "how would I do that?"

My friend said he'd talk to the coach, and then also suggested that I join him at a summer wrestling camp he was signed up for at Annapolis, at the Naval Academy. The coach talked to me, made a call, and got me signed up. That summer I spent a couple weeks learning to wrestle under the tutelage of a champion wrestler and coach named Peery, who just loved to use me as an example to wow the class with fancy moves.

During the stay, there was this dorm hall monitor, a snarky little college student we called "Douche Miser" because he called us all "Shit Misers." He seemed pretty alright for the whole program duration, and he'd tell dirty jokes, and act like one of us, and let us get away with shit.

On the last day of camp, I had missed breakfast because I got up late, so I was the only one in our hall, other than him, who was still packing. DM announced he had to make "one last round" to make sure everything was in order, and would I like to join him. I said sure, no reason to think anything was off, he was cool right? The first couple rooms he asked me wait in the hall while he did his check and let him know when the others started to return, then he came out and we went to the next room.

I just sort of stood there not really paying any attention to anything in particular, just zoned out, when he walks up to me with a wallet in one hand and some cash in the other. It very much just looked like someone coming up to give you money to get them a coffee on a Starbucks run or something.

He chins up at me and holds his hand out. I wasn't even thinking, just followed suit, and he slapped a five dollar bill in my hand. I stared at it, looked up at him. Dumb as a board.

"Thanks, man – you're a great look-out, that's for you." He chuckled and tossed the wallet back where he got if from. "Come on, a few more rooms left... nobody sposda be back for 15 minutes..."

I knew it was wrong; it was disgusting to me that this dude who was so much fun the past weeks was nothing more than a dirtbag. I shook my head side-to-side to make sure this shit was actually happening. He turned to go about his assholiative activities; I shook my head a few more times, and turned and walked out in the opposite direction.

When I got to my room, I grabbed my bags, and noticed I still had the money in my hand. I had no idea what to do with it. Did I put it back in the room, wait for the kid who it belonged to, and say what happened? Did I go try to tell someone who was an adult and hope they would take care of it? I knew how adults viewed me, and DM was a clever little bastard; he'd spin it and I'd be on the losing end for sure. I mean, it was only *five bucks*, right?

I left it there in my hand, grabbed my bags and split. I was at the pick-up area outside in the parking lot half an hour early when my buddy Jeff showed up. He asked why I left before saying goodbye to everyone. I couldn't tell him. I felt like shit.

I folded up the fiver three or four times and jammed it deep into my wallet. It stayed there until my wallet fell apart Senior year, and it stayed in every subsequent wallet I owned until I was in my late twenties or early thirties. At *that* point I gave it to someone on a street corner asking for change, when I guess I'd finally had it as a grim reminder for long enough.

I owned my part in that whole transaction, but it and other similar interactions taught me a valuable lesson about trusting my own instincts, and not taking things on face value. Yeah, I headed in the wrong direction for a lot of years, just always assuming and expecting the worst whenever *anyone* was introduced to me as being in authority; but then you grow up and realize that a large portion of any interaction is you, and what you do with it.

So you give folks a chance. You deal with *anyone* long enough you'll figure them out. *Anyone* can hide behind a facade for a short period of time, but at some point... *They* show up.

Try to have a little courage, and turn away when you need to. Don't kick yourself too hard: kids can be stupid, confused, or scared, but you will eventually learn – and hopefully *all* it will cost you is five bucks.

Eggs are now up to like six bucks for a dozen... more depending on the store, location, and type of eggs. You get Heirloom Eggs in a Trader Joe's in Las Vegas, they are gonna run you 37 bucks a dozen. For eggs.

They aren't even Fabergé. Just normal – with the exception of the Heirloom ones – chicken eggs.

Chicken.

Eggs.

What is that even supposed to mean? Is that like an egg that's *so special* you pass it down from generation to generation? Just make your omelette and shut up, poseur. *Heirloom eggs.* Just call them what they are: really expensive common bird eggs.

When I was a kid we had chickens for laying eggs. Maybe 30 at most, depending on the time of year. I remember when we first got them as chicks, and I'd think about when they would start laying eggs. Nice clean, white, perfectly sized, egg-shaped eggs. Laid gently, one at a time, in a neatly-arranged, perfect, clean little straw nest, to be collected by us kids every morning and evening in a Toto-basket lined with blue gingham, or some such.

In one of Life's perfectly orchestrated "expectations-meets-reality" lessons, I got schooled.

Turns out, chickens don't give much of a shit about neatly-orchestrated egg laying in bespoke nests. At least ours didn't. They'd just drop 'em anywhere they liked most of the time. On the ground, on the roost bench, outside by the fence, in the feed trough or water tray. Oh, and sometimes even in the nice wire-mesh-bottomed egg-laying boxes attached to the wall in the coop for *specifically that reason.*

And "clean," "white," or "perfect size and shape?" YeahNO. I remember the very first egg I found; I wasn't even sure it was an egg. It wasn't egg-shaped, at least not chicken-egg-shaped. Maybe viper snake-egg shaped, kinda ping-pong ball round. It was light bluish in color, had an almost translucent semi-hard shell, and it was covered in chicken poop.

Most of the eggs we got had some degree of poop on them, you know, what with cloacae being and doing what they are and do. Wow. That is a LOT of bi'ness to be happening all in one location, what with the in-coming and out-going, and breakfast-production. Never mind where meat comes from, if some folks saw where eggs come from, saw what they looked like "fresh," well, more people would be eating caviar instead.

We had so many eggs we couldn't eat them fast enough. And I'm talking about two parents, later two grandparents, and four kids, at least one of whom ate like he had stock in Food in general and got a residual check every time he scarfed down an entire box of Cheerios for breakfast. We could EAT. And yet we still couldn't eat them damn eggs fast enough.

Chickens it seemed, could not get enough of two things: laying eggs, and crapping all over the place. Which, due to a government design situation, were both done in the same body location, out of the same hole.

So, we'd frequently get a few dozen eggs a day, we'd eat most, but the rest had to go somewhere, and that somewhere was to other people. And the person who was voluntold that the job was his to make those eggs go away, was me.

I remember when we first noticed that we had a surplus of eggs; my dad came home one night from work and noticed we were getting a backlog of those little square-ish blue-gray cartons of eggs in the kitchen. We didn't use the "regular" two-rows-of-six-eggs-each cartons like you find in the store.

Our cartons had three rows of four eggs each, and the tops were either blank or sometimes had this "STRICTLY FRESH!" stamp on them. The eggs didn't need to be refrigerated, they really don't need to be in order to last a long time, just make sure you flip them once a week, they'll keep awhile. Of course, refrigerating them makes them last that much longer; and if you flip AND refrigerate, well, I'm sure they could last a million years.

The Chinese even have their "Thousand Year Eggs," that I assume, namitalically speaking, are at least a thousand years old. They sure look and smell that old.*

One way or the other, Dad wasn't keen on finding out how long those backlogged eggs would last.

That night, and it was dark out by then, he grabbed a paper A&P grocery bag from the pantry, shoved it in my face and said

"Don't come back until they're all gone."

I looked up at the stack of cartons, maybe six or eight of them. I looked back over my shoulder through the picture window in the kitchen out at the dark street, its one lone street light making a pool of light just big enough for every cutthroat, jackboot, and werewolf to be able to see me clearly as I trudged up and down the street like some sort of sad little Flower Girl trying to make pennies a day to keep coal in the hopper so she didn't freeze to death.

I looked back up at Dad, whose face was not budging one fraction of a bit, then I started to pack the cartons into the bag.

---

*And taste like they could be; we got some one time, I ate them, no one else in the house would. Cowards.

The bag alone weighed enough – maybe ten pounds empty. Each carton of eggs felt like it weighed six or seven pounds, depending on how many double-yolkers were in each, and how thick the shells were. I mean, there was some math you could do to figure all that out, but I was just a kid. The whole bag/carton get-up was roughly 87 pounds, I know it.

Then I put on my threadbare coat – handed-me-downed from two brothers before me – and I dragged my soulless body out into the night where I was sure I would perish before my mission was accomplished. I really did feel like that submariner in that U-Boat movie, where Matthew McConaughey tells him,

"You go down in that bilge and DO... YOUR... JOB... SAILOR," knowing that he'd die doing it.

Now, I was a pretty sharp kid, regardless of what my brothers and sister would say out of jealousy. I knew exactly what I had to do to get home in time for whatever was on TV, say C.H.I.P.S. or Adam Twelve or something, I mean I was trying to find the TV Guide Magazine when Dad cornered me; but whatever... I was prepared to do it.

"IT," of course, was chucking all those eggs out into the woods, or perhaps seeing how far I could hock them into the lake by moonlight. However, I was also smart enough to know that if I came home too quickly, Dad would know something was up, especially when he asked to see all the money.

The money. SHIT. I had to have proof that I sold them. Goddamnit. They weren't a lot, mind you, this wasn't the 2020s, not for another 50 years yet. Our dozen eggs, in their societal-norm-shattering three-rows-of-four-each (or really, if looked at from a different perspective, four-rows-of-three-each) blueish-grey cartons, with an attention-grabbing "Strictly Fresh!" emblazonment on them were maybe fifty cents.

I think there were lines on the lid for Grade and Size as well, but what kid knows from Grades and Sizes at 9 years old? A few hours ago they were still on the inside of a chicken. There wasn't any other way to get a fresher egg unless you squeezed the chickens right over the pot of boiling water, and TRUST me, there was more than eggs coming out if you did, so you did NOT want to do that. Wash the eggs, situate them nicely into the carton, then brag about how fresh they were... all for just 50 cents. Grade and size? Pssshhh.

I'm not even sure what a carton of eggs from the store cost back in the 1970s, but when I was 9 or so, there was a recession and an "Energy Crisis," and eggs cost more than a gallon of gas... like maybe 75 cents. So come on people, 25 cents off fresh eggs RIGHT OUT OF A CHICKEN'S ASS? You couldn't afford NOT to buy them. Arbitrary Grade and Size notwithstanding.

But on *that* night, as the shadow monsters played about me at every turn, (there weren't actually any turns on that street. It was pretty straight in the mile I walked down and back) I sold nary a dozen. I glanced down to the dark waters of the lake on my way home, thinking about just chucking them all into it, followed by my own body just so I wouldn't have to listen to the barrage of bellows when I got home with the same count of cartons I left with.

I mean Jesus, it was like 8pm or something, everyone was asleep, this was a farming community. We all had to be up at 2am to collect even more eggs and slop the pigs and stack firewood and dig holes and shit; who the hell was up at 8pm waiting for the Neighbor Kid to swing by with fresh eggs?

So this was the story I built in my head as I went back home after – quite frankly – not knocking on one freakin' door in the 20 or 25 minutes I was gone: "no one was up." Surely Dad would believe that. Ha ha... HAHAHAHHAHAHAHA, I laugh now even writing this. "*Dad would believe that.*" Good times.

Anyway, I got yelled at as expected, I took my licks and liked it, and I was still in front of the TV to watch Squad 51 without missing a second of the exciting theme music. Of course, I capitulated to making sure I sold them during the day starting tomorrow, and I did get my ass out there and I sold 6 dozen of them.

One of our neighbors, the next house over to the west were family friends, The Oberman's. Mr. Oberman, or "Sparky," as he was called (I was dying to know later in life how he got that nickname, though I surmised it was from his personality, always smiling and laughing) would have parties at his house all the time in his basement, and he came over frequently when we had one. He loved his beer, surprise surprise for not only a German but also a German who lived in that area of nowhere. Overall, we – or at least I for sure – really liked the Oberman's.

One night, Sparky came over, already about three steins in, and dragged us all over to his place, Mom and

Dad had beer and whatever food was being grilled, us kids had White Rock sodas. For some unknown reason, Sparky took it into his giant, bald head that he was going to teach me how play The Spoons.

"You know how to play The Spoons?" he grinned at me, about two and a half inches from my face, the Grolsch rolling into my nose on waves of words. Then he grinned wider and produced two metal spoons from somewhere on him, I did not dwell too long on the "where."

"C'mon, I'll show ya!" he laughed, and he sat down and showed me how.

I played, I actually played. I mean it was not exactly Rocket Science – or even Egg Sales – but I achieved a certain level of proficiency in mere minutes.

Sparky's wife wound up buying eggs from me every week. Two dozen eggs every Wednesday afternoon. She would pay me with two shiny Kennedy-head fifty cent pieces each time, a lot of them were "solid silver."* Now I didn't have a great idea of the value or significance of silver fifty cent pieces at the time, but I had a vague appreciation for them thanks to my mom's father who collected coins. So I saved the silver ones and spent the others.

By the time I left the Adirondacks, I had a nice pile of silver half dollars. Through moves and the erratic spending habits of teenage boys, by the time I was

---

*"Solid" being a misnomer, as these coins were in actuality 90% silver and 10% copper.

married and we had our first child, I still had more than twenty left, and I had an idea of what they were "worth" as well. That worth was what I had in mind one day when, living on the tiny paychecks we had with a new baby in a tiny town in Arizona, I tried to find a pawnshop or coin collector to buy them so I could get formula for the kid.

But it was late on Friday, everyone was closed, and wouldn't reopen until at least Monday afternoon. And we were BROKE at that moment in time. So I took my fancy silver half dollar collection to the grocery store and bought formula, ground beef and ramen for what it was worth – ten bucks at face value.

The kid running the register eyed them with a greedy smile as I counted them out; he knew what he was buying out of the till later that night. Lousy opportunistic punk.

My daughter to this day gives me shit about not hanging onto to those coins for a little longer, and frankly I kicked myself enough over the years about it as well. The thing that mostly gets me today though, is: I would only have been able to buy one and a half dozen Heirloom Eggs with that pile of coins today at face value. At the highest point in their perceived value with collectors, I probably could have bought a *really* nice car.

All said and done, though – I'm glad I didn't hock all them eggs into the lake that night when I was a kid.

THE WILL TO SURVIVE

SIGH.

Well, the day is here.

I had a feeling it would get here eventually... just not so soon. There were things I could have said and done to mitigate, but... blech. If "could'ves and should'ves" were "documents and notaries," things might be different. But, no. They aren't. And worst of all I know it's all my fault. Whatever the case.

I haven't got the will to survive.

Literally.

I have not created a Will yet. My oldest brother has, and he's already rubbed THAT in my face. All his "I'm an adult, and I do adult things" bullshit.

"I had a job for thirty years... I retired from a job... I have a Will for all my STUUUUUUFF..."

What a show-boat.

He knows that his Will will make sure his Stuff survives a major Life Event. Not even sure why it is called a Major Life Event when it is the exact second that all Life Events get deleted from OutLook, and your calendar is now free and clear of events, responsibilities, compromises, travel, appointments and everything else.

Oh, you may have one more trip to the doctor, though it may not be your family doctor or the one who is in-network contracted to do your check-ups. But it will be a trained professional, who – let's face it – may show up drunk to do your last exam. It won't matter, because you'll hardly feel a thing, and this person faces zero consequences of screwing something up. He or she could literally leave half a dozen rusted hemostats in your chest cavity, and nobody would say boo.

Unless you have that Fake-Deadness, like that character in that Twilight Zone-type show had. Where everybody *thought* he was dead, but he could *hear* everything around him, and he could *feel* it too. He was about to have a REALLY bad afternoon.

But then he cried, like a big baby, and everything was all right. Yeah, *you* won't have *that* issue. I'm pretty sure that is like a, maybe, one-in-thirty-seven chance kind of thing. So just let that thought go, Greg. Get back to the matter at hand. Your Will.

Just to let my wishes be known, though – this one-in-23-chance Fake-Death thing, THAT is why I want to be cooked when I die. I am NOT going to be one of those unlucky souls who has to lay there getting his innards ripped out and his blood drained, and his lower jaw sewn up to his upper jaw, and has to FEEL the whole thing because nobody bothered to check brain activity before they did any of that nonsense.

I mean good God, wasn't that Twilight Zone-type show enough to enact the Check-Their-Tear-Ducts-for-Saline-Before-You-Cut-Them-Up Act? Why hasn't that piece of legislation been porked through Congress yet? Paper-clipped – nay, *stapled* – to the other stuff about Blue Pills and Free Guns?

You'd think there would be a LOT of politicians worried about being fake-dead-eviscerated-and-buried. I mean, you can clearly see some of them are very likely already pretty Fake-Dead sitting in their chairs neither quite awake nor nodding-off asleep as the Speaker drones on and on. Does no one care?

Anyway. Cremation for me, please.

I don't even care if I suddenly wake up in the oven and pat my palms loudly on the cardboard lid, just push the green button.

I have been pro-cremation for a great many years now, but in actuality, this has simply been because there really weren't any other good options to plain old burial/interment. You either get cooked, or you take up space in a landfill, or get tucked into a REALLY heavy, concrete bureau-sock-drawer of Eternity.

When I start to think about some sort of above-ground cement junk-drawer-as-final-resting-place solutions – I'd almost rather be buried underground. At least underground, when you wake up from Fake-Dead Syndrome, you may be lucky enough to break through the lid, because you just *know* your kids/spouse went cheap on the box. Plus, you spent the last few months of your life learning and perfecting the One-Inch Punch, so BAM, lid breached.

Then it's just a leisurely crawl through the newly sprinkled earth, which, YES, you simply push back down into the coffin, filling that space, which gives you THAT MUCH space to work in the soil above you. Then you just keep going up to the surface, scooping soil from over you, then shoving it behind you. Just like a *Mowdie*; Hilts and Ives proved this works, so don't let "experts" gaslight you. Scoopin' n shovin', shoving' and scoopin' – then you're out.

And six feet? Horseshit, six feet. Maybe in the movies or TV it's six feet down.

When my dad was interred in his gold-wreathed sarcophagus, and when that first back-hoe of soil went in, it dropped maybe a foot and a half onto the lid. So, this isn't even an all-nighter we're talking about, from breach of lid to fresh air, you're looking at like six minutes tops. Eight if you happened to lose an arm like my Great Uncle Joe. Pretty sure he was real-ass dead when they buried him though, but you get the idea.

Anyway, the whole above-ground-concrete-filing-cabinet thing. You see it frequently in movies, where the body that no one bothered to check was still alive or not is ceremoniously shoved into a cold gray box of thick cement junk-drawer, pre-filled with phone charging cables, old birthday candles, chopsticks, and condiment/sauce packets.

I mean, think about *that* for a minute. Just THINK. You wake up in there and you are HOSED. Ain't no One-Inch Punch breaking through concrete. Don't even think about screaming to let anyone know you're still alive in there:

"GAAAAAHHHH... I'M STILL ALIVE! IT WAS FAKE-DEAD SYNDROME... like in that Twilight ZONE-Type show!"

Concrete is NOT as easy to hear through as soft, freshly-dug earth is.

Even *if* they heard your cries, when they try to open the drawer back up to pull you out, that fuckin' potato masher gets the drawer stuck, and that's IT. Game Over. Nothing anyone can do now but leave so they don't have to be traumatized from your agonised screams. No sense in two (or more if they had the presence of mind to call the fire department) people getting freaked out from your tortured screams and dying from mental anguish.

That's why I need to work on my Will. To let everyone concerned know... OH! I just remembered. They have other choices now than just cremation or trauma-inducing holes above or below ground. I almost forgot.

Over the years they have developed new means of disposing of your *actually* dead body. Anything from seed-pods so you can grow into a tree, to mashing you so hard you turn into a diamond, upper-atmosphere dispersal of ash from some sort of NASA-launched spaceship, and even composting. Of course, as usual, the wealthier you are the better service your carcass gets.

James Doohan, from Star Trek, actually was able to be smuggled aboard the International Space Station by a 1%-er. That's right, it was a Secret Mission, flown by a non-astronaut to take Scotty's remains into space.

My brother knew at least one real, actual astronaut, who had to go through the Air Force, then trained for years, and met all sorts of rigorous physical and mental standards before being allowed to fly into space and carry out important Humankind-expanding work on the ISS.

Turns out, all you *really* need to do is make a LOT of money designing and building Computer Games, and have a friend who makes so much money in marketing that they are able to build their own rocket. Then you, too, could take a celebrity's ashes into space.

Does anyone else NOT see the problem there? *Seriously*?

Okay then... exactly *what* do you think is going to happen when the cat they keep on the ISS to keep the mouse population down, chases a mouse up on the mantle of the fireplace, and knocks that urn of ashes down and those ashes go *everywhere*? That shit is like beach sand.

Unlike Scotty's remains, however, beach sand doesn't make a 72 billion dollar Space Station short circuit, lose orbit, and crash into a sheep meadow in Azerbaijan when it gets into your personal, privately-owned cracks.

Billionaires, they just don't think about how their actions affect others.

Which is why I think if it becomes more affordable by the time I kick, I would like my first choice to be composting, and my safety disposal method is now cremation.

Cremation is great, except – and ONLY – as noted above; however, it doesn't really do anything to give back to the biome that has so unselfishly given to me when I was actually alive. Ash, being the lowest form of broken-down material on the Earth, has nothing more to offer the planet: no nutrients, no building blocks for anything else to grow from. Unless you are a Phoenix.

Burial, same thing. Assuming they check to make sure you are *really* dead, they suck out your blood, they replace it with, what, sawdust and Twinkies to preserve your body? What exactly is that all about? Why would you need to be preserved? So you can take up space for a longer period of time in a landfill?

And stop that, it IS a landfill. It is the textbook definition of LAND... FILLED-in... with YOU. Never even mind the metric tons and square acres of stone monuments that could be better used to make aqueducts and meeting halls and things that help society and those left living.

Composting. Now *that* allows you to contribute even after death.

They have come up with a process wherein they gently place your body in an OSHA-approved tube (like a giant fancy cigar tube with a screw-off top) on a comfy bed of wood chips, grass trimmings, kale, and maybe some paper and cardboard – so you feel like you're just out resting in nature. And then they dump a few orange, five-gallon Home Depot bucket's worth of nightcrawlers, mealy worms, and blowfly larvae over you... and let relaxing, serene Nature take its course.

A few weeks later, your granddaughter shovels you into the bed of green beans and corn, gently works you into the soil, and presto: your family eats you by proxy because you are now inside their vegetables. You are giving back. You are nourishing those who come after. And maybe some neighbors, because let's face it: your granddaughter can only eat so many you-infused fresh green beans.

ONLY downside: becoming poop later. Potentially clogging the toilet. Then the tears start all over again when your family – after already letting you go in some funeral home – now have to bawl as they plunge you down the septic system again.

My *secret* third option, which would be so awesome if my family could swing it, is Sky Burial.

Sky Burial is kind of nifty. It is a ceremony in Tibet where Monks feed your body to vultures. Read that again if you like. It is a CEREMONY, where MONKS FEED your BODY to VULTURES. Circle of life. This method gets you back into the biome a LOT quicker than even composting.

First, there is a "Body Breaker," whose job it is to... well... just picture the Chef at any Benihana Grill, dicing and chopping up vegetables, making fried rice, crafting a volcano out of onions, and flicking bits of food into customers' open mouths. Translate *that* to the professional who gets your body ready for the Bearded Vultures. Whole body is gone in like 15 minutes. GONE. Carried heavenward by the winged scavengers of God.

Worst that could happen now is perhaps one vulture ate a Vegan at the last meal, and had a bit too much roughage, so you end up on the windshield of some tourist's Honda CR-V in the parking lot at the Sky Burial Gift Shop. Not to worry, there is probably a homeless gentleman at the next light who can take care of that with a squeegee. Creating jobs... AFTER death.

I really love the idea of this means of disposal, but again I fear my family will go cheap, and instead just drape me over one of the platform bird feeders in the side yard where the blue jays and doves and squirrels will just peck away at me for months during the day. Possums and skunks, maybe the odd silver fox, may nip at the carcass at night, then the sprinklers come on at 2am and the whole thing is just a sloshy, gooey mess. You have any idea what the lawn guy will charge to rake THAT up and cart away? He charges 20 bucks per bag for leaves.

All of this to say, I really need to get my Will together, because like Celine Dion, I need to know that my Stuff will go on. I just cannot stand not knowing what will happen to all those screws, washers, wire nuts and drywall anchors in my little blue metal, clear-plastic-drawered shop box after I die without a Directive. It HAS to go on to someone, get USED. SURVIVE.

I would literally die if my wife and kids were able to say – "SEE? You saved all that shit for nothing."

DUMB LUCK, OR BULLETPROOF

Ah youth. What a great stage of life. Sure, being a little kid is fine and all: so very little responsibility, so much attention. But young adult to teenager is where it was at, man. We could be only halfway good-looking, and just by being young we were already attractive. Everything was new, nothing could stop us.

We of course knew everything at that age, too. Adults were dumb and oppressive... we were smart and gorgeous and bulletproof. Our poor guardian angels must have been working overtime every freakin' day, though, because we did some *absolutely* dumb shit.

Some things were only mildly dumb, and turned out to not be life-threatening at all, just sort of poor decision making. Like Hammer Pants. Or walking home from wrestling practice with my friend Jeff.

It wasn't a very long hike, and we usually needed the aerobic exercise anyway to cut weight and boost our stamina. It was a straight shot a little over three miles down Big Bethel Road, across two highways, but some of it was very rural at that time: tall grass, trees, undeveloped land.

On one stretch of overgrown road, there was this *really* run-down shack, for lack of a better architectural term, that looked like it was built in the early 1800s. There was almost never any activity around that shack, it looked like any movement at all would send the sagging roof crashing down on whatever ghosts still lived there.

However, on one particularly hot day, there were these two old gentlemen sitting in rockers on the front porch. Old, like they probably built the house, old. Rocking themselves with canes pushing off the gray sun-bleached porch floor-boards.

"Hey boys, whatchu doin' out in this heat?" One asked as we got close. His voice sounded like someone who regularly power-sanded the inside of his trachea.

"Whyn you g'won inside, git yaself a grip soda anna moon pie?" Said the other, a tad more energy, same gravel-and-broken glass voice.

"Yeah, g'wan in gitcha grip soda inna moon pie," the first repeated.

At first blush, these two appeared to be some sort of animatronic robots from *Westworld* meets *Chuck-E-Cheese*.

We immediately looked at each other and understood the look to mean "this is how murders happen."

But the two gentlemen seemed very insistent that we avail ourselves of a grip soda and a moon pie each, and apparently we were not real bright. Very little traffic, no one would see us go into the building, and we never told anyone where we were or when we left school – we just walked home frequently.

What the hell? It was hot, we were bulletproof, and what could possibly happen that we couldn't handle?

We walked up to the building, and it and the two gentlemen looked a LOT older up close, if that was possible. Yeah, we mos def could take them in a fair fight.

"Twenty five cent each. G'wan in, leave the money onna counter," they enticed. Seemed they weren't physically able to go through the whole Rube Goldberg list of actions that it would have taken to stand up and walk us into the Kill Room.

On the other hand, that was *exactly* what serial killers would do in that situation. Disarm with age and folksiness, then bar the doors and windows from the outside, while their kin made short work of us in the grip soda aisle. Clever, had to give 'em that.

"Sho is hot," Number Two commented as we stepped up on the porch between them.

"Yeah, no kidding," I said, as I opened the door.

Inside was like a mausoleum dedicated to snack and comfort foods. The whole shelving situation was like a shrine to bygone days: the goods they sold sure would not have been found in the Piggly Wiggly or Big Star, at least not with *those* expiration dates and prices. Pretty sure there was a thin layer of dust coating absolutely everything.

"The soda back in the ice chest," Number One rasped from out on the porch.

How convenient, we have to walk through the snack cake graveyard to get to the soda. We looked at each other again, shrugged, walked to the back, and sure enough, there was a large plastic cooler on a table – and it was full of ice and canned sodas... most of them Grip. We grabbed a soda each, walked around a bit until we found the Moon Pies – what I used to call Scooter Pies growing up in the north – in an open box near the front counter, the individually wrapped treats stacked neatly inside.

There was a coin tray on the counter, no cash register. The thin cardboard box was the bottom portion of some larger snack carton that had been unevenly cut with a pair of scissors or a number of short bursts from a dull utility knife, with a few coins in it. We dropped fifty cents in each, popped our cans and enjoyed the cold, dark purple drink as it cooled our throats. A few seconds to make sure we were not poisoned, then we walked out.

"That ice cold soda feel good, I bet," said Number One.

"You ain't lyin'," chimed in Number Two. "You tell ya frins, now, hear?"

"We will, thanks!" we said as we stepped off the porch. I am not sure what the cost was at a regular convenience store at the time for a grip soda and a moon pie, but sure bet it wasn't fiddy cent. And it sure wasn't anywhere near as chock full of character as that broken down building that those two old friends decided to turn into an oasis on a dusty stretch of road half way between the school and our Base Housing.

We stopped there frequently over the next year and a half, same two gentlemen always on the porch, same little carton-tray full of coins on the counter, but it got less and less murdery with each visit. It was NOT gonna be the next hang-out, not for our generation anyway, but it had its charm.

Our big hang-out was Heritage Square, a shopping center on route 17 out in Yorktown, a short distance from us. York High was one of our rival/sister schools. All the locals who grew up in the area either went to York or Tabb High, sometimes both if they moved or one school got overloaded. Other close-by schools were Bruton, Poquoson, and Grafton, and we frequently wrestled or scrimmaged with all of them. So we knew a lot of students from these other schools, and in general we got along.

Sometimes we ran afoul of people we did not know, like this huge guy in the McDonalds in the square one night. There were maybe seven of us wrestlers getting McRib sandwiches when they were new. One of us, 98 Lbs, had ordered first and went to find some tables for the rest of us. When we got over to him, he was standing nose to chest with this rotund local who was maybe in his twenties, drunk, confused, and just itching for a fight.

The other six of us fell in behind our friend against

this girthy individual, who kept insisting that he "wanted to dance" with our friend. None of us knew what his deal was (though Moonshine was an option), not even 98 Lbs, who said he did nothing to provoke the encounter.

We just looked at each other and thought, is this guy serious? It's one (albeit very large) person against seven wrestlers. I was no fighter, and neither were one or two others, but there were seven of us... it wasn't going to end well for his side.

Fortunately for everyone involved, Big Guy's friend walked back in, and took a few minutes to get him to understand the same. Big Guy eventually was coaxed away by his apologetic friend, but his eyes never left 98 Lbs for a second as he backed out unwillingly. It was great sometimes, knowing that most folks knew the shorthand that you didn't mess with wrestlers, because you never knew what you were going to get.

Of course, sometimes wrestlers got in their own way because they figured they were invincible. Some weekends we'd get BB guns and wade through the swampy land in Poquoson with friends, trying to find crabs and other little critters to shoot (yeah, I know). And all we really got was stuck in muck up to our thighs, hoping we could get out before the tide came back in. That would have been hilariously ironic if we'd been stuck in that mud and goo when the tide came back in, and gotten eaten by crabs, muskrats, and alligators.* Blissfully ignorant.

---

*There have been sightings of alligators in Virginia.

Although the fault would *technically* have lain with the wildlife swamp critters in *that* scenario, I do acknowledge a slight amount of responsibility on our own behalf for the soggy fate that could have befallen us.

Unlike another water-related event at the tail end of our Senior year, where the entirety of our deaths would have been squarely on our own shoulders.

The day of Graduation, Tom, Rob, Mark, and I went out to spend the day on the beach at Fort Useless (Fort Eustis), which looked out onto the James River, west of the peninsula we lived on. Unlike the swamp in Poquoson, east of the peninsula, which was a gateway to the Chesapeake Bay (which was really just a fancy boutique name for the Atlantic Ocean).

We oiled up and lay on the sand soaking up as much sun as we could so that we'd be tanned or burned or some hybrid by the time we walked that night. When we'd had enough sun, we went for a swim, though not real sure how much swimming we did, at least not me or Tom.

Now, I knew I was not what you would call a "great swimmer" at that time. I loved water, but the actual motions and buoyancy that constituted "swimming" per se, yeahNO. I believe the more correct term would have been closer to "non-swimmer."

Did that keep me from going neck-deep in the James? No. No it did not. I went out as far as I could with Mark and Rob, which was quite a distance, as the river floor there was not a particularly steep grade. They were happily splashing around as I just sort of waved my arms around underwater to give the impression I was treading water. A pretty decent cover, I thought to myself, who would know?

Tom, however, stayed on shore and shouted teenage male things at us; I couldn't hear most of it in actual words, just tone and inflection. It was copacetic, until Tom decided to start throwing stones at us. Tom was strong. He could throw stones of a pretty good size quite some distance, say, far enough to reach my bobbing head.

Here's the basic trouble with thrashing arms around underwater vs *actual* swimming: actual swimming makes you pretty mobile and agile in the water. Walking with your feet on the bottom does not. We've all done that slow-walk/slog in a pool or lake or ocean, right? The deeper the water, the harder it becomes to get your legs to move fast... running is completely out of the equation even at waist deep.

I was neck deep. Rob and Mark easily avoided the visible stones being hurled at us, and it became a sort of game for the three of them. The problem started when Tom grew tired of trying to hit moving targets that were farther out than I was, and turned his attention and aim instead to the non-moving, fake water-treading floating head that was me.

By the time I noticed his aim was getting REALLY good, it was too late to try to "run" to get out of the zone. When a fist-size stone hit the water a few inches in front of me, I was getting worried.

"Okay... you win..." I shouted, "knock it off, man."

He threw one last stone, and I'm pretty sure it grazed my hair as I ducked underwater enough to get out of the way. I awkwardly breast-stroked my way closer and closer to shore, and finally came up out of it soaked and pissed.

"Dude, what the HELL?" I shouted at him.

"Why didn't you just swim away, dumbass," Tom asked, like it was somehow *my* fault.

"I can't swim that well, you idiot!" I shot back.

"You can't swim?" he asked, surprised, "Who lives on a peninsula and can't fucking swim?"

"I didn't see you in the water," I said.

"That's because I can't swim... but at least I stayed out. Who's the idiot now?" laughed Tom.

Yeah. Yeah. Yeah, I could not get around that logic. Nicely played, sir. Dick.

Boys, right?

We drove back home in Rob's Gremlin, stopping to grab some McRib sandwiches at Heritage Square, our heads now filled with the impending last few hours at Tabb High. We talked about the trip we needed to make in two days down to North Carolina.

A friend of ours from the wrestling team, Kenny, a few grades below us, had just recently lost his father to cancer, so his mom was moving back to be closer to her family. We had all offered to help pack and move them that week.

On the morning we started the trip, I was riding shotgun in the Gremlin, and Kenny was in the back seat. We were right behind his mother's car and the Uhaul. We headed out on Big Bethel Road, and were stopped at the light on 134. Between the funeral, graduation, summer plans, moving – we had a lot going on. Our minds were all over the place as we started across the intersection again.

Lost in these thoughts, I absent-mindedly looked to my right as we crossed the far side of the intersection – the north-bound lane of 134. If this were a movie or some TV show, this would have been what you call "the T-bone Shot" inside the car. You know that shot: it's at an angle where you can see the driver and passenger, but you can also see enough of the window that you *just know* some shit is gonna happen in the next two seconds.

It did.

I saw the Buick LeSabre a split second before the thing hit us going fifty miles an hour. I don't think the other driver was able to hit the brakes much. I vaguely remember seeing their face, very likely looking every bit as surprised as I would have been, had my head not been in the clouds.

When I became aware again, and things started to move at normal speed, I was sitting on the edge of a ditch, being asked questions by a paramedic, like what was my name, what was the date, and where did I live.

I was good on my name and date, but the "where do you live" gave me pause. I actually didn't have a place to live at the moment. My mom was supposed to be leaving the same day to head back out to Las Vegas, as we had moved out of that base housing months earlier. I wasn't going to be in Virginia for about a week with the move, and I guess it just slipped my mind that I was staying at Mark's for the summer when I got back.

To state the obvious, details were groggy, and this may have passed for head trauma.

By some divine intervention, everyone was in pretty decent condition, including the other driver. I got the worst of it, having been sitting at the point of impact. I ended up at the hospital ER; I had a subdural hematoma the size of a grapefruit removed from my right elbow, a handful of stitches there. My left leg made contact with the underside of the dashboard console, opening a big ol' gash there that needed more stitches. The eggplant-colored bruise from my knee to my foot lasted two solid weeks.

I was given pain meds and something to stave off infection, and was told to rest a lot over the next few days.

Other than that, the doctor was surprised that I was so generally unscathed. We all got off *real* easy on this one. I got dropped off at Mark's house with the meds, and took a nap.

Following the doctor's orders to a T, Mark and I went to a party later that night, I felt fine. Had bandages on my arm and leg, but other than that I was good to go. People didn't believe me when they asked about the bandages, and in fact we kept hearing a lot about what great shape we were all in over the next few days, people shaking their heads when I told them we were in that accident they had heard about. The looks on their faces puzzled me. Until I went to get a few things out of the car in the police impound lot a few days later.

HOLY. SHIT.

I just stopped dead and my jaw dropped when I saw the Gremlin. How the HELL did we walk away from that pile of twisted and folded metal? The car was almost bent in half at a 45 degree angle. The front passenger side area was obliterated, the now V-shaped passenger-side door jutted in toward the driver's seat.

That poor old Gremlin was a nightmare, and all I got was a few stitches and some bruises? That was insane.

Flash forward to 2024... I woke up this morning, put my sock on wrong, and was limping for thirty minutes with a crippling foot cramp.

I tell you what... when you say there ain't no substitute for being young, bulletproof, and watched-over by guardian angels working overtime... you ain't lyin'.

IF
IT
BLEEDS,
WE
PROBABLY
STABBED
IT

"Our liberty depends on the freedom of the press, and that cannot be limited without being lost."

— Thomas Jefferson

"The ethics of journalism are one of the most important factors that make a journalist credible."

— Judy Woodruff

"Good journalism gives people the information they need to live their lives. Great journalism takes it further, giving people the tools to change their lives."

— Cory Booker

"To be a journalist means to expose yourself to danger, to face criticism, to confront power, and to stand for the truth."

— Anna Politkovskaya

The Fourth Estate: the term given to the News Media – Printed or Broadcast – denoting a power block in society. The Press was able to organize and put forth ideas (very specifically in a political arena) that could, would, and did shape and change the way things have gotten done. To put it plainly, they could spin what information got to The Masses like the Dickens, man.

The original Three Estates came from a French idea prior to their Revolution of 1789, as to how they saw society being divided up. The First Estate was the Catholic Church, or religion in general; The Second was Nobility – the rich fancy folks; and the Third was basically all the commoners, both the Riff and the Raff – you and me.

As one might imagine, while the Third Estate contained the vast majority of the population, it held very little power when it came to how things actually got done. You know, unless you count the whole torches-and-pitchforky Revolution thing. But look how long it had to go on before they turned on the One Percenters, who *really* should have listened to The Doors more when it came to thoughts about guns and numbers.

In "modern" times (1840) Thomas Carlyle (an Historian) wrote of Edmund Burke (an Member of Parliment):

"Burke said there were Three Estates in Parliament; but, in the Reporters' Gallery yonder, there sat a Fourth Estate more important by far than they all."

All this nonsense could be, and indeed was, learned in college in Journalism 101, wherein a great reverence was instilled in students who wished to take up The Pen as would The Knight take up The Lance to defeat The Dragon of Ignorance in defense of The Truth.

Those who attended institutions of higher learning with an eye toward a career in the Wordly Arts were indeed thinking of the welfare of others, and not themselves. Heroes, really.

Me?

I had very little idea that I would ever become a writer, journalistically speaking or otherwise. I started out as an Anthropology Major, then switched to Sociology; I had a very vague view of college as a *real* thing. Now, I did have *some* idea of what college was about IN GENERAL, I mean. I had seen *Animal House* 15 times, so yeah, I knew how it worked.

But MY idea what college looked like for ME varied greatly from what it probably SHOULD have looked like; if it were up to me alone, I may never have had the chance to write anything other than a paper on Courage in Ms. Ream's English 101. However, as the saying goes: Some are born great, some achieve greatness, and others just wanted their cartoons printed for all the world (campus) to see.

And so it happened, while reading the student newspaper one afternoon on a lumpy couch in the student union, I noticed the complete and utter lack of humorous drawings. As this was something smack-dab in my wheelhouse, I walked up to the office and asked if I could get my comic strip in the paper.

I wound up working for the *Yellin' Rebel* in a few different positions, starting out as the staff cartoonist, after submitting my comic strip that I started in high school. The fascist editor at the time – aptly named Franco – wanted me instead to do editorial cartoons that he would dictate. In a compromise, I drew his editorial cartoons and he printed my comic strip. I was on my way to pissing off a lot of students and university administration alike.

Pretty soon I was writing and drawing my own editorial cartoons, hitting the Basketball coach (Tarkanian), the Board of Regents, various upper-level admins including the President of UNLV (Goodall and then Maxson). Franco loved it; he REALLY enjoyed stirring the pot and provoking. He was a great teacher.

I moved my way up to writing some feature stories, covering campus events and general humor, and got to double dip – recording the stories live on the spot, writing a version for the paper, and submitting the recorded version to the radio station, *KUNV*. Both the newspaper and the radio station were the only offices on the third floor of the student union at that time. The third floor was more like a rectangular peninsula that jutted out over the food court below. One side looked out through the 20-foot-high glass walls of the multi-purpose room where the Student Council would hold its meetings. The other side looked down on the door to a huge auditorium where class registration, dances, guest speaker talks, and films took place.

When we got bored some days, and there was a Student Council meeting going on, we would stand on the balcony and shout stupid things down at them, like Dustin Hoffman's character at the end of *The Graduate*, with similar effect.

The radio station's DJ booth door was about ten feet away from the back door to our newspaper production room. The nature of both the jobs, and of students in general, was such that we made a lot of friends between the two media giants. Weekends, especially late at night could get interesting. Between the sleep-deprived shoulder-chipped paper staff and the alt-rock post-punk pre-grunge music format, and the crowd that visited and worked at the radio station, it was nothing short of diverse.

I rather enjoyed a lot of the music they played, and the DJs were kinda fun to chat up. Soon I and a few other newspaper staff had a little radio show we recorded there, a sort of sketch show with a mish-mash of humor pretty indicative of the demographic.

One night, pretty late on a weekend, I was working at the newspaper, getting it ready to go to press. I was alone for a few hours, as the rest of the skeleton crew had to go do things for a bit – homework, get some sleep, make a food run, get laid etc.

One of the more interesting DJs, Romney, walked in the back door to the production room and asked me if I could cover him for a few minutes until he got back from a "very important meeting" he had at 2am on a Saturday night.

I clearly stated

"Man, I can cover you for 30 minutes AT MOST. If you can get back by then, I got a paper to put out," I reasoned with him.

"Yeah yeah yeah yeah yeah, man, shouldn't take me more than 15 minutes. Twenty tops, it's right across the street," he fast-talked me.

I eyed Romney.

Romney poker-faced the shit out of me.

Little back story on Romney. The first time I met him in person, was at the newspaper. He was a cartoonist and sometimes columnist like me when he started, but I knew he also worked at the radio station. One day, in the middle of the afternoon, he lumbered his huge frame into the office with a briefcase, sat at a computer to write a column, and clicked open the sproingy latches on his case.

Then he proceeded to take out a fifth of Popov vodka, a small bottle of orange juice, and a glass, and mixed himself a screwdriver... the whole time cackling like a mad scientist. He sipped his drink while he typed. Those were the entire contents of that brief case, by the way. Well, that, and some drawings scattered haphazardly, rattling around with loose pens.

When I finally succeeded in creating a full page of comics in *The Yellin' Rebel*, Romney's work was at the top of the list, his shit was weird, and I dug it.

He was a bit of a wild card though, as nice a kid as he actually was. I liked him, we all liked him... but when the weed was whacking, he could be, I don't know, a bit of a handful. I doubled down on my stipulation:

"Dude, if you are not back in under thirty minutes, I throw on *We Are The World*, and it plays until you get back. I shit you not, man." I said firmly.

We Are The World was pretty big then, having just come out recently, and played on every station in town and across the country. However, the novelty had run its course, and now everyone was just tired of hearing it.

"Awww come on man," he pleaded, "come OHHHHNNNNN."

"You said it was a short errand. You have thirty minutes. GO." I said, and I walked out the door with him. I turned right toward the booth door, he turned left and I soon heard the cavernous echo of his stompy flat feet skipping two stairs at a time as he galumphed the three stories down the concrete stairwell.

His play list was easy to follow, can't remember it but I'm sure it was all This Mortal Coil, Elvis Costello, Adam

Ant, Joy Division-y, he knew his shit and could usually put together a list for any program the station had. So I played what he had lined up, didn't say anything on-air to dispel the illusion that "The Rocket" (his nickname) was still sitting there in the booth.

DJs always kept an ear out wherever they were so that they knew what was going on in the booth. The station Suits did the same. As long as nothing objectionable happened, the suits were okay. If a DJ had to make a run for something, they'd put on some long-playing stuff, run downstairs, hop in their car, crank the radio up, and haul ass knowing exactly how much time they had to grab their bag of weed and/or nuke their burrito at the 7-11 across the street.

So when Romney wasn't back in :30 exactly, I got on the mic and said

"This goes out to Romney, my man, something new, hope you dig it," and I cued up *We Are The World.*

At three and a half plays I heard the stomping of heavy, scrambling feet echoing back up the stairs, and the slam-and-shudder of the loose metal door at the end of the hall. I got up and walked out of the booth and passed Romney as he scurried – smelling like a skunk – to get into that chair and stop the madness.

"GODDAMNIT, maaaaan!" he blurted.

The phone in the booth was already ringing when I walked back into my production room. Apparently someone had woken the station assistant manager, and she wanted to know what was going on. Romney had a learning moment about time management.

In short-order, I became production manager at the newspaper, and then, with some effort, was installed as editor. Mind you, I really didn't want to be editor, I just did it to piss off the student government and a few of the fraternities on campus – with whom we, the newspaper staff, fought constantly about what was to be printed in the paper.

As far as editors were concerned, we were keeping a bit of a dynasty going within our cadre of pot-stirrers and nose-thumbers, and it was my turn to run. I ran on a ticket of "he was a cartoonist and production manager... how much harm can he do?" and I got massaged through to the position, which I upheld like a drunken monkey with a pen and an axe to grind. To be perfectly honest, during my reign, I was often drunk, I did have an axe that needed grinding, and pens were my best friends.

My (perceived) pissy attitude was in some ways beneficial as Editor, because I got to write provocative editorials every week to bring to light important issues for discussion. But mostly I enjoyed poking the President of the University, a new gentleman by the name of Robert Maxson, who, by the by, was from Texas.

"Booooohb," as he like to be called – it felt folksier – had the drawl, the tallness, the whole Texas vibe, and he was incredibly easy-going on the surface. The newspaper was always dealing with him and the Chair of the Communications Department, Dr. Barbara Cloud.

Now, the problem with me (one of many) was that I was a young male who had grown up on *Animal House* as perhaps my soul informational input to university life.

And I *soooo* wanted my UNLV experience to be like THAT. Well, minus having to join a fraternity.

So I was constantly striving for *THAT* level of campus life. The *Yellin' Rebel*, our newspaper – OUR newspaper – did a yearly salute to Yellow Journalism, where we lampooned and skewered public figures and policies, and maybe took shots at others as well, such as a specific fraternity that we were always at odds with. Maybe even a State Senator, Congressperson, or Board of Regents member upon occasion.

For my *Yellow Rebel* installment as Editor, I ordered a full-page enlargement of a photo of Bob, from his official UNLV headshot used in all marketing. Due to an error in the specs sent to our printer for halftones,* we ended up with a poster-sized version of Bob.

We did what any college students working at the student newspaper would do such a situation: we taped it to the wall and used it as a dartboard. Only we didn't have a lot of darts. But we did have a lot of X-acto blades with the smooth, cylindrical, silver aluminum handles (paper production was still mechanical paste-up with galley strips on gridded paper flats).

On any given day there were half a dozen of these admin-budget-purchased highly necessary tools of our trade stuck in Bob's face on the wall, and embedded into the sheetrock behind it. There were also – because

---

*A halftone was the print-ready photo created by a process back in the days before digital publishing where – if you've seen them – photos were turned into black and white art via tiny black dots.

weekends were long hours – a few of these blades stuck in the acoustic tiles of the ceiling.

"Why?" You may ask?

Simple.

We found out if you laid an X-acto in your palm and swung your hand up swiftly – AND deftly, you could get the blades to stick in the ceiling.

One Monday, Bob had occasion to visit our offices to try to gain some clarity as to why we did a Particular Thing. Since I was Editor, that Particular Thing in question's responsibility was firmly on my shoulders, as the mature adult in charge.

Bob walked – nay, he had a way of swagger-sauntering when he walked – into the office where I happened to be, and came right up to me

"Mr. Dooooooahchak," he drawled, "just the man I need to speak to about this P'ticulah Thing that happened with your newspaper this week."

We worked on production Fri-Sat-Sun, and took the flats to the printer at 6 in the morning Monday, then picked up the papers later in the afternoon and distributed them around campus and a few just-off-campus places. The paper could not have been out for more than a few hours when he visited us.

Bob kept unwavering eye-contact with me the entire time, as he explained the Administration's views on the Particular Thing that occurred. With a Texas-friendly smile that said "Imma kill you if this happens again, son," he asked a lot of open-ended questions such as,

"Is this the sort of thing that makes the university look good?"

and

"How do you think this makes my life – more, or less complicated?"

and

"I'm sure you and your staff had nothing to do with this, did'ya now?"

and then the oddly precise,

"I have no doubt this can be fixed by some easy means, like picking up the remaining papers and destroying them, and perhaps a call to the Person's Office that this Particular Thing affected and making some sort of sincere apology, wouldn't you agree?"

To which I offered some heartfelt "yes sirs," or "I couldn't agree mores," or "I will make sure nothing like this ever happens againses," to each question.

When he was done, he sized me up, offered another, broader, toothier smile... and then something caught the corner of his eye. He turned his head for the first time since he walked in, gazing to his left... where he saw himself with an X-acto blade in his right eye, one in his left temple, and two in his chin.

He gazed for three seconds or so, looked back at me, looked over at my Managing Editor who happened to be my soon-to-be wife (who also usually had to be my mouthpiece, voice of reason, and ersatz Jiminy Cricket), and then turned to leave.

That was when we all heard the clank-and-tinkle of something metal hitting the concrete floor.

Bob turned back around and we all looked down to see the X-acto blade that had fallen from the ceiling right between us, still rocking.

Bob looked up, saw another blade stuck in the ceiling, shook his head in a sad manner; perhaps he realized the dollar value of the instrument (as well as the acoustic tiles), and hoped it hadn't been damaged in the fall. He sighed, and then walked out.

All in all, for what happened, he was amazingly pulled-together and generous, for a disappointed parent-figure.

That Particular Thing? Seems what happened was, a state senator had been featured in our newspaper for some senatorial blah-de-blah he was doing a week ago, complete with a picture of him addressing a large audience. He was wearing a really nice suit.

On the left lapel of that suit, somehow a number had appeared in bright white. Three numbers actually, all the same, and right next to each other. Some may think the juxtapositioning of these three numbers might make reference to a Great Evil; it's all very unclear.

Also unclear was how the numbers came to be. I mean, we certainly were not responsible; Bob had said it himself. We were all adults there. Except for me, who was still legally a teenager, and my soon-to-be brother-in-law, who was two years younger.

I know it looked bad, but coincidentally, we also

happen to be the ones who put that page together Sunday night, and may have had been up for like 26 hours straight, and that may or may not have lead to shenanigans, and things that seemed really funny at the time.

Using sound logic, there is the distinct possibility that a consensus had been reached that the numbers – apparently etched into the photo with an X-acto blade – would not reproduce because they were not black like the tiny little dots in the half-tone of the senator's picture.* It's all conjecture and hyperbole, I mean there was no way to tell what transpired. All moot now anyway, all injured parties have since passed on.

Bob called it, though, and we did what we knew to be right. We blamed the folks at the printer. Rather we blamed the fraternity for getting at our flats after we dropped them off.

We took the direct-line number from Bob and made the call, threw the printer staff under a bus, then requisitioned a UNLV truck and picked up the thousand or so existing papers and yeeted them into a dumpster, re-half-tonized the photo that "the printer had messed with," and reprinted the paper at our cost – which was also the University's cost.

And we never spoke of it again (in reality, we laughed about this all the time).

---

*This is hard to believe, because if you scratch a half-toned photo, the scratches show up as white, the color of the paper. What were those vandals thinking?

I am reasonably sure that poor ol' Bob had a few ulcers named after us, and there was absolutely no wonder as to why Dr. Cloud had so many issues (if you'll pardon the pun) with us as journalists.

Or why that one Fraternity always tried to get us fired when the Student Council sat to discuss student activities and policies.

It was not the first nor the last time Bob had to deal with fabricated issues involving this particular batch of staff – who, by the by, were around for about four years in some way or form, as my soon-to-be-wife, a good friend of ours, and my soon-to-be brother-in-law, all had turns at being editors; two after me, the other before.

We would be targeted quite often over the course of our reign of terror. Most of the time for stupid little bullshit; to wit, when we went out one night and ran around campus tearing down all the campaign flyers for a certain Fraternity member running for Student Council. Sorry, allegedly, *someone* ran around campus, hiding in bushes until the campus police had passed in their rounds, then ran up and tore the lovingly, yet spitefully-stapled flyers off the cylindrical notification columns and stuffed them in the trash barrels nearby.

Heheheheheheh... it was us.

But, MAN, did we make good poster-tearer-downers. The time management skills alone that were involved in working at the newspaper and then taking a few brakes to cover the entire campus doing our misdeeds, that was a skill not taught in the Humanities Building.

In point of fact, if facts were, indeed, involved, we tearer-downers learned at the feet of the Masters... the very same Fraternity who did tear down the posters of the Newspaper staff member that was running in the same election.

When by chance, we did get illuminated by the bright-white beam of the campus police car's spotlight, we managed to outrun the po-po through a series of evasive maneuvers through the buildings in the dark, that could only have been described as "Centipede-like" (Google the video game), until we found our way to the ground floor rear entrance of the Student Union Building, clicked the mechanical push-button lock code on the door, and escaped up the stairwell back to our offices.

Thinking ourselves as some sort of Avenging Spirits in the Night, we had a good laugh at the campus cops once we were safely back in the office. Chuckling and shit-talking

"Ha ha ha," shit-spake we, in great jest "what a bunch of losers! What were they going to do if they caught us, anyway – arrest us for cleaning up the campus? Ho HOOO!"

To which the campus cop – who in true Popeye Doyle fashion, had followed us up the three flights of stairs to our evil lair, snuck into the offices, and had been listening to our self-congratulatory, highly incriminating super-villain conversation the whole time – replied

"How about destruction of property, criminal behavior, theft of goods, and a few others?"

"Oh, yeah… all that," we almost certainly thought to ourselves. But to that cop, we only responded

"What? Officer Lonnie, what brings you here tonight?" Coupled with two of the most innocent face-looks EVER.

A few well-placed questions from the Accused were rapid-fired back at the Boy in Blue. Solid questions about the burden of any proof, shadow of doubt, habeas corpus, in flagrante delicto, and the coup de grace "what about the Fraternity that tore down OUR flyers?" seemed to have him reeling in his Florsheims.

"Just knock it off, okay?" he said, smiled, and left.

Officer Lonnie wound up having a close relationship with the Newspaper from then on.

But we were *definitely* on Double-Secret-Probation from then on. DEFINITELY.

Animal HOUSE!

Ba-DAH dahdah DAAAAH DAH

ANIMAL HOUSE!

A WHOLE LOT OF WORK FOR NOTHIN'

I am always fascinated when I drive through the countryside and I see those little family burial plots in the middle of nowhere. You know the ones, the little 100-200 square-foot fenced-off pieces of shrubbery-overgrown land, maybe has a nicely-spread tree shading one or two really old headstones. If you find parking and you walk over to them, the once-smooth-cut headstones now look like some sort of pumice stone you'd sand down your heels with, and the dates and names on them are barely-legible at best.

"Ernst Hochleighter, husband, father 1823 – 1868" and "Judit Babics Hochleighter 1830 – 1901"

Firstly, you will notice the wife lived longer. Quite a few years after the ol' man passed away. She clearly got a second chance at life, after Ernst dropped dead behind a plow and two bony, fly-encircled horses while tilling up the hard-packed sod for the Nth year in a row, stubbornly hissing at poor Judit,

"NEIN, I know ziss year vill be bettah!"

Maybe he was playing the Long Game. Maybe he knew his years wouldn't amount to anything, but perhaps he was thinking that *some day* someone would live on that land, and it would be a better place because he had prepped it, picked every field stone out of the ground and built a wall with them.

A sun-tanned, wind-blown Judit could only wipe at her forehead with the back of her calloused and deeply-lined hand like some sort of GIF made from a Dorethea Lang photo, and continue chucking lumps of prairie sod into a pile for later use in the family fireplace to stave off freezing to death in January. Probably muttering under her breath the whole time.

Ernst just would not let that shit go. Twenty years of growing rocks and weeds, eating rabbits and whatever-the hell-*that*-thing-was he shot the other day. Weaving dolls out of coarse prairie sod for the youngin's, and sawin' on the fiddle every Sunday after their Lord's Day feast of roasted Whatever-*That*-Was.

Whichever way it went, *somebody's* prayers were answered that scorching day in 1868. And as great a relief as that was to Judit… she STILL went ahead and got buried next to Ernst thirty something years later on that little family plot out in the middle of that hard-packed earth.

Wow.

I mean, Judit wasn't a bad-looking woman, handsome by all accounts, strong as an ox; which makes you wonder why Ernst didn't hitch her up to that plow and let the horses rest now and again. She could have had any life she wanted after that. Could have gone back to the big City of Rumpkin's Crossing and got her a job School Marming. I know she could have marmed the living crap out of that school.

But there they lay, thirty years apart, in a weedy patch of prairie sod off 183 just north of the airport. You will notice that the kids wanted no part of that. Effram and Dorcas saw the shit their parents went through. Effram kinda really resented the fact that he was, in fact, the third Effram that Ernst and Judit had. Apparently they just kept naming their sons Effram until one of them lived through the winters long enough to help with the rock farm. So THAT name meant nothing.

No, Effram and Dorcas went back to Rumpkin's Crossing as soon as they were the age of majority, 12 and 9 at that time. They worked at Harrison's Notions till they saved up enough money to move Back East, where they attended school, made something of themselves, and disappeared into history, hopefully in a much more respectable bone yard covered in a better class of heel scrapers.

What a life.

I had a cousin I was particularly fond of, we had the same sense of humor, and whenever we talked on the phone or in some text app, it was always effortless and fun. Her father was my father's brother. And they were all tall. My uncle was six foot one or so, my cousin wound up six two, and her brother even taller. I wound up with my other side of the family's genes, maxed out at five eight and a quarter on a good day after Pilates.

My cousin, like her father, was an artist; whereas he worked in oils, she worked in jewelry and wool. She designed and made custom jewelry and soft sculptures from needled felt wool. REALLY nifty stuff, just as high-end in quality as anything you'd pay out the nose for on Etsy or some street craft fair.

She was also a writer. She wrote a series of fantasy novels that were quite well-written and interesting, just not my bag.

When she was younger she lived in Philly for a bit, drove a Hack. Not a taxi cab motorized vehicle, but the horsey-drawn kind. She traded that in for a Harley later, and she tooled around with her S.O. hitting biker rallies, once coming through Texas and leaving a rally immediately before a very violent brawl broke out.

But somewhere in there, she wound up with some serious health issues, I think she once said it started with an extreme growth spurt in high school, which took her up to that six-foot-plus height she carried so well. Thyroidery. And then something else, and something else, and then some *things* else.

She bounced from doctor to doctor, pill regimen to pill regimen, nobody ever really able to properly or correctly diagnose whatever the hell *that* was and how to effectively fix it. A lot of years of just exhausting issues. I really felt bad for her – despite the fact that her sense of humor didn't seem to ever waiver, at least not when we talked.

Then finally one year she had a really bad episode, and she had to get choppered (the helicopter kind) to a better hospital over the mountain into California, where some clever doctors found out what was going on. They fixed this, sewed up that, took *these* pills away, gave her *those* pills instead; then put her on a long list for a liver transplant. She got bumped up to the catbird seat of that list, quickly got a new liver, and was doing well.

The last time I spoke to her in the hospital, she sounded great, and was on the mend. We had to stop laughing because she didn't want to pop any stitches. She said she was going to make a felt sculpture of a comic strip character I created years ago, and I was going to paint her a goofy raccoon picture. She was home soon, and we had a few more chats online or by phone.

I did the painting, but for some reason I never sent it. Well, I knew why I never sent it... because I was a procrastinating lump sometimes, and just kept putting it off. One week I kept saying I should ping her and see how she was doing. Two days of that nonsense went by, and then I got an email from my aunt, her mom, saying that my cousin had passed away suddenly a day or two earlier.

This was at the tail end of Covid, so going to a funeral would have been iffy at best. But her family was not big on pomp-n-such. No funerals, no flowers. No long obituaries. Like her father, she passed from this world quietly with no fanfare. Just kept shoving that gol' dang plow through the hard-packed earth for years, making the world a better place than she found it via today's versions of Prairie Sod Dolls.

Jesus H, what a whole lot of work for nothing.

MASOCHISM CALLED, THEY SAID DIAL IT BACK

I am a big proponent of trying to figure out why things happen. Anything from why I just HAD to stub the shit out of my toe right before I had an audition, to why mosquitos seem to wait until you're half asleep before they start their strafing raids on your ears. And for that matter, what is so damn special about *your ears* to them?

A slightly more existential question that plagues me to this day, is why some people just keep on doing things that clearly aren't working or helpful, despite many

many years of data that provide a great deal of sound argumentative points *against* doing them.

We, as humans, are taught – or rather we learn – quite early on that when you stick a bobby pin into an electrical outlet, you will get zapped.

We've all been there, amiright? You're unsupervised in your room at age four, and you find one of your mom's bobby pins on the floor, so you immediately make the connection that "plugs go into the wall and power things, so it stands to reason that if I plug myself into the wall, I will gain more power." Right? RIGHT?

Anyway, I did it.

It was the dawn of the Fuck Around and Find Out Era with me, which only lasted to somewhere into my 50s. I ain't *that* slow. But you know, in my defense, there is a good likelihood that one of my famous hindsight theories is correct, that my mother left the bobby pin there on the floor precisely to teach me about the world.

The second, MORE likely theory, is that my father found self-elimination had fewer repercussions to his career than tying me in a burlap sack and tossing me into the lake, under the pretense of "teaching me valuable survival skills."

Whatever the case was, I did indeed find a bobby pin*, and I did indeed jam it into a socket on the wall of what was to become my oldest brother's room.

---

*By now you should have Googled what a bobby pin is, so let's assume we're all on the same page.

The feedback was immediate, and well-taken. I had learned much.

The great thing about being four when you do something like this is that your motor skills and upper body strength are not particularly fine-tuned enough to allow you to hold on for dear life once the pin is inserted. Dear Life is actually looking out for you – if you are lucky – and yanks your body backward, where it gently lays you out on the cold linoleum floor, so you can relax, and think about what brought you to this particular *mise en place*.

Experience then seeps into your body via the pores in your skin that were suddenly enlarged and cleared out, or some other psychic connection with the Universe, and you come-to with a New Plan as things pertaining to electricity and its proper usage.

Easy peasy, shocky freezy.

If only the rest of your life worked as well with the lessons that were to come. But it seems that only very – shall we say – *fairly* incomplex concepts actually teach this way; not true, useful, intricate Life-Long Lessons.

- Mouth off to a kid bigger than you?
  Blood is released from your nose.

- Try to pet an unknown quantity dog?
  Get snapped at.

- Break virtually anything in the house?
  Dad puts your head on a pike as a warning to the others.

Simple actions. Simple conclusions. Lesson learned. It does not happen again.

When, exactly, in life do we lose this ability to learn quickly and permanently so that our lives don't become one long, dreary wake-up-on-the-cold-linoleum lesson? It seems like when we get to be adults, we go from a very short math equation to a never-ending hamster-wheel of similar information being hocked at us but not sticking as quickly or as permanently. I.e: being taught a lesson that we may or may not actually retain and use.

It starts with asking people out and always getting Friend-Zoned, and ends somewhere years later with trying ad nauseum to "grab that dream and win."

High School feels like the spark on the fuse for this powder keg. You (in my case, me) ask a girl out, she says

"No, sorry, I just really value our friendship too much to go out with you."

And you back away in horror and embarrassment, cocking your head and asking yourself

"Did I read the signs *wrong* on that?"

But then you pretty much just turn around and try again with Jennifer over there, and she smiles and says

"I think we should just stay friends, thank you though."

And as you reel away from that, you bump into Betty, so you ask her out, and she just paraphrases from the memo

"No. Friends. Bye."

That's enough to get any normal, level-headed human being into a train of thoughts that One should never, under any circumstances, ask someone else out.

But, no; you do it five more times. Because there were signs, and flags, and nuances, and your friend heard from the buddy of one of her class-mates that she really liked you, so how could this, as well, be doomed to failure?

And yet, it was.

Eventually, *way* longer than it took with learning about burning your finger on the stove, you may catch the drift, and you just stop asking girls out. Period.

In college, perhaps you start out wanting to be an Anthropology Major, with dreams of all manner of Indiana Jonesery being in your future. But turns out, most Anthro majors just end up sitting in a dark basement unwrapping and categorizing rocks, most of which are probably fossilized poop, and you never see the canvas tent of an actual dig site.

So you change to Sociology and/or Psychology, because, let's face it, how difficult can *people* possibly be, right? But they are.

And then you move on to Journalism, and then Radio/ News, and maybe one other boring, bullshit, do-nothing major right before you finally settle on a degree in The Arts just so that you can get your stupid degree, like say in Film, which in your defense, sounded like a nice way to skirt the dreaded English or Philosophy degree.

Then, after college... the real trouble starts. You have this idea in your head of where you "belong" and you have now heard so many stories about folks who have "stuck to their dreams no matter what!" that you feel that you *have to* – in order to not be labeled as a "quitter," – just keep trying until you make it.

You can *feel* it... it's *sooo* close...

And this time you never learn.

From there on out you are sticking an indeterminate amount of Bobby Pins into an infinite number of wall sockets, and you come-to on the Cold Linoleum of Experience, wondering why you can't quite feel your fingers. And for some reason you simply just can not stop doing it; and the lesson takes longer and longer to sink in.

Your cranial lesson-sponge is just jammed full, and you find your ability to make good judgement calls has simply "gone away." I mean you got a degree in *The Arts*.

You quit your job at the Widget Factory and decide you want to do something that matters, so you take up writing, or acting, or painting – anything The Arts-related. Okay, you settle on acting, because that lasts forever. Your face forty feet high on the silver screen, *that* is truly something that matters, right? I mean, you know you were just *born* to do that.

You take the classes. You get the headshots. You brood and smolder just camera-left of the lens. You take every background artist gig* that you can, you are told this is The Ladder you climb, so you climb it.

---

*"Background Artist" is just euphamistic for "Extra." You are an extra piece of that scene, meaning you can be cut out on a whim.

What they won't tell you, is that each and every rung of that ladder is not only soft rubber that stretches down when you step on it, but is also coated with a thick layer of "Nos" that extend like spikey, sharp spines that tear at your hands and feet. While you are busy shredding your palms and soles, Mike Tyson has been hired to belt you in the face through the spaces between the rungs, three times per space.

But you keep climbing. You slip backward a few times; you may have a burst of energy and skip a rung or two as you launch yourself upward. If you have any discernment at all, you notice that you pretty much end up on the same rung of the ladder year after year. Heroically, you are certain that if you try just a *tiny* bit harder... you will make it. You think about how great it will be when you get to the top of that god-forsaken ladder, where you *deserve* to be, where you were *born* to be.

"By God, I WILL MAKE IT! I HAVE THE TALENT! I HAVE THE ABILITY, I HAVE..."

BAHHHHH-BAAAAM! Mike Tyson's right hook catches the entirety of the front of your head.

"Shut up, bitch," he mutters in a high-pitched snarl, "Get off already."

You see some of the *biggest* stars you have ever seen circling your head. Those stars, in turn, are seeing a bunch of tweeting birds surrounding *their* heads. And the birds' eyes are so swollen shut, that they can't see anything as their little talons flail about, trying to jam their tightly-clutched bobby pins into a wall socket.

This goes on for years, more years than it should, because you no longer are able to tell time. You simply drive yourself forward, believing, *knowing*, that Your Time is next. With a sickening, sucking squelch, you pull your hand up from the spikes that run through it, and grab the next rung up, *one... more... time*.

Your other hand has to reach down and help lift your leg, which winds up separating and leaving your foot stuck in the thorns on that rung. Ironically this actually helps you, because the thorns on the next rung can't penetrate the bone nub on that leg now.

Suddenly – perhaps in a moment of clarity, maybe a hallucination brought on by Tyson making toothpaste out of your lower jaw – you decide that, well, the hell with it, I'm just going to go back to work full time at the Widget Factory, and be happy doing that. I'll come home at night, have dinner, drink a few beers while I watch The Game, or some sort of Ethnic Bake-Off show, and that will be my life... as I calmly and patiently wait for my heart attack and the sweet, peaceful embrace of the Angel of Death.

Trouble is, the Widget Factory is now making Digital Widgets, and the workforce – what's left of them anyway, 'cause there had been a reduction in force – has started to resemble children. By next year, Widgets won't even be needed anymore.

You look around for other "normal" work, but there isn't any, because it's all disappearing, going digital, or only hiring people who won't actually know what they are doing.

You find that you have managed to outlive the job you learned so well over the years. So reluctantly, you turn back toward that Arts Ladder you had been trying to climb.

But now you notice it's no longer a ladder, but a stainless steel Stripper Pole. Wrapped in barbed wire, and slathered in active napalm and nuclear waste. Mike Tyson is still there though. He beats his gloved fists together a few times, taunting you forward

"What are you waiting for, crybaby?" he squeaks frighteningly. "Git on it."

You sigh heavily, and trudge lifelessly over to the pole and try to climb, as Mike sends your gall bladder shooting out the right side of your body.

"Thorry," he says, "they thaid I'm only thposda hit you in the fathe. The pole throwth me off."

You shrug. Tyson shrugs. Like it matters. You climb. You do this until you die.

This is what it is like to have a life in The Arts.

This is also why I was never allowed to speak in my kids' classes on Career Day.

MUSTANG DREAMS

What cars start with P?

Pontiac, Plymouth, and Ford.

What does "FORD" stand for?

"Found On Road Dead," or "Fix Or Repair Daily"

You know why they named the company "Ford?"

Because "Steaming Pile Of Shit" didn't fit on the oval logo.

For the longest time, my Dream Car was a 1964 (1/2) Ford Mustang. Cascade Green, hard top, bucket seats. I just absolutely loved the way that car looked, very distinct, very fast *looking*. The first Mustangs looked like what would happen if you bolted tires to a flexed bicep and then branded a galloping horsey on it. Easy to spot with the grill, the famous tail lights and gas cap... it was cool *ad bosseum.**

By the time I came on the scene of being able to drive, let alone buying a car, the brand was 15 years old and there were already quite a few variations out, not all of which retained the cool or provoked the drool... I'm talking about YOU, "Fastback" (apologies to Steve McQueen).

But I still wanted one of the originals.

There was a kid a class or two above me named Roger, and he actually *had* a '64 Cascade Green Mustang... but his was a convertible. Man oh MAN, did he look impressive whenever he drove it to games or dances.

A group of us kids would be out chatting in the parking lot, we'd hear that engine roar, and we knew Roger was pulling in. We'd stand there, our hands stuffed in our jean pockets, necks craned – because our bodies were frozen in position – to see that bad boy slip into a spot near us.

Roger sold that car to a junior when he graduated, and it was my dream to be the next in line to buy it when this new owner graduated. But that *jag* kept the car instead of doing what I wanted. The absolute *nerve*.

I kept my sanity by telling myself the fuel filter would

---

*I know the 289 engine did not quite meet the standards for being a BOSS, but I liked the Latin play on words.

probably pop some day when he was on the highway in the middle of nowhere. Spiteful? Yes; but I was a teenager who had been wronged.

As a soon-to-be Senior, I was indeed in need of a car though, and so was my sister, who was also a soon-to-be -Senior.* ** *** We had jobs we needed to get to, and the house currently only had one car, which our mom and stepfather were usually using for work.

It was the car we drove to Virginia in, and the first car I learned to drive, and drove for the remainder my Sophomore year when I got my permit and then license: a 1976 Chrysler New Yorker. Gangrene Green, 37 feet long, 129 cylinders, 600 gallon gas tank, seated an even-dozen people across the front bench seat. This was the kind of car where you didn't look at the speedometer to see how fast you were going, you watched the gas needle.

Even back in 1980 it took a wheelbarrow full of money to fill the tank, and if you wanted to get up to speed on the highway, you had to pull out of your driveway at about 62mph and never hit the brakes between your house and Hwy 64. Once at highway speeds, there was no physical way to brake that 12-ton chunk of tank metal in time to hit an exit, so you had to work it out to where you'd run out of gas as your exit came up, so you could coast to your destination.

---

*We were not twins or anything, I was just smarter than her.

**This statement has not been verified at the time of printing.

***We will just assume it is true for the remainder of these essays.

You may think I speak as though I hated that car, and you would not be far from the truth. The only actual redeeming feature about it, was that you could hit a brick wall doing 70mph not wearing a seat belt and still walk away unscratched.

Fun note: My very first "car accident" happened about three hours after I got my license. I picked up my buddy Mike to go for a spin in the old Tanker, but we had to get gas first, so it was off to the 7-11. We pumped 81 bucks worth of gas (which would get us to Heritage Square 5 miles away), and then I went to pull up close to the store to run in and pick up some Gatorade and Andy Capp Hot Fries for the trip.

As I pulled into a spot right up front, I banged into the bumper of a car right next to my intended parking slot, completely unable to determine the distance between us because depth perception had no use on a New Yorker. As luck would have it, the owner of that car was just leaving the store and saw me do it, so little chance of backing out and parking in a new spot.

I got out of the car, nervous as hell, thinking I'd lose my brand new license. The man never even flinched, he just looked my car down and back, glanced at his car, and said

"You're alright."

He got into his car and drove away. As he was pulling out, I noticed he was also driving a Chrysler New Yorker, the solid Krypton-steel bumpers evenly matched on the 2mph nudge. Nobody was getting dented. Crisis averted.

Our Chrysler did go away one day, and was replaced by a '75 Mustang II, a bit worn-in, but a fun little car to drive. It got paired up for a short time with a rust-bucket '67 Mustang, three-speed hardtop that my stepfather's brother gave us to look after while he went overseas for a few months. My stepfather tried to teach me to drive the '67 a few times. I *really* did not take to manual transmission manipulation. I nearly got us creamed when I failed to negotiate the articulation and hand-eye-foot coordination needed when pulling across a four-lane highway in one smooth motion. It was more like a series of fits and starts, with the fits winning eight-to-one. In all fairness to me, the clutch was sloppy as shit and that car was a death trap to anyone but the owner.

I was not allowed to drive that car again... rather, I did not *allow* myself to drive it again.

One day, while driving to my job at Busch Gardens, I passed this strip mall where folks would park cars for sale right near the street. On this day there was a new car for sale... I immediately pulled in and looked at the rear taillight, and there it was, a shiny Raven Black 1964 Hard top, 289 V8. Interior was immaculate, not a scratch on the outside. And best of all... it was an automatic.*

The only major deterrent: the price tag. At $2500 bucks it was not only out of my price range, but it was also a few hundred dollars over the original cost of the car. I learned a lesson in what dreams cost rather quickly,

---

*I realize this might seem like a 50% reduction in Cool Points, but shut up, who asked you? I ALMOST DIED.

as my $125/week paycheck started to wheeze under the strain I had just attached to it.

Every day I drove past that lot, I checked to make sure the car was still there, and it was. Until some a-hole bought it out from under me about three weeks later. BOY, did that hurt. If I was going to get a car, I mean WE... I know, sister, blah blah blah... were going to get a car, we'd need financial aid to get it quicker than we could afford on our own.

So, our stepfather said he'd help us with the money; all we had to do was find a car, and he had to approve of it, he wasn't going to shell out for some falling-apart shit-bucket.

My sister and I looked high and low, but could not find a nice one anywhere. Truth be told, I know for a fact my sister did not give two craps and a whistle for a Mustang; in fact, I am not entirely sure what it was she did want, but I do know *her* dream was not in sync with *mine*.

We had finally found a car we could agree on, when we passed a car in a carport with a For Sale sign on it. A 1975 Maverick, a rather nice consolation prize for missing out on The Dream, I thought. The car was pretty sound mechanically, the owner was eager to sell, and the price tag was not bad... but it was 500 more than our limit according to our stepfather.

We asked the owner to hold it while we drove home to see if we could put the squeeze on our money guy – and he actually said yes. Good car, good price, here's the money, go buy it.

We sped back down the road to the Maverick's house; he was only fifteen minutes away; so the whole round trip from him to our house, haggle time and all, was less than an hour. We showed up, the car was gone. Someone else had snapped it up minutes after we saw it. I was PISSED. I may have called the owner a dick.

Another valuable lesson learned: the one about Money Talking. Like this *fine citizen* was going to wait for two teenagers to ask mommy and daddy if they could buy his car. Dick. He was a dick.*

The car shopping got downright tedious after that, and my sister and I would shop independent of each other frequently. She would look at cars with her dumbass boyfriend, who she said "knew about cars;" (*pssshhh*) while I would look at *actually* decent cars at a fair price that would not only be mechanically sound, but get good gas mileage, and might also get me laid.

And then one day, the worst thing imaginable happened.

My sister had found a car and convinced our stepfather that we both agreed on it... and she bought it.

"I'm sorry... WHAT?" I asked, my face not hiding the pained look at all, head cocked to one side, one eye squeezed shut.

"Yeah, it's outside," she said.

We ran outside and my heart sank to the bottom of the

---

*He was a DICK.

Marianas Trench. There in the driveway sat a 1974 Renault. It didn't even have a color, more like a *suggestion* of a color. MAYBE it was light blue? Light Bleau, more like. Light BLAHHH. Oh my god, what a piece of crap.

We argued. She stated we needed a car and she had gotten one. I countered with one could not honestly, with 100% accuracy, call that *a car*.

A French vehicle built as an afterthought. What a fantastic metaphor for giving up. It was made out of aluminum foil. The single-ply doors were so lightweight, you couldn't even slam them when you were angry because the car wouldn't start. And it wouldn't start – not even exaggerating here – 75% of the time.

The only saving grace out of the entirety of the "car" was the kick-ass radio/tape deck it had. I scratched my head many times wondering what went through the previous owner's mind when they installed an after-market high-end radio/sound system that clearly was worth more than the vehicle. My guess was hearing crystal clear accordion music while smoking a clove cigarette in your beret was *la plus haute importance*.

In the end, resistance was futile, and the car came with a (rightly so) "Le No-Backsies" policy. We were stuck with it. I made the best of it. My friends Eric and Lauren invented "laughing out loud" when I pulled up to get them to go to the mall. It was a rolling embarrassment. I wound up naming it Ralph, The Wonder Car, because you would always wonder when and where it was going to die on the road.

Would you like to know when and where it died on the road?

The second or third time I drove it to Busch Gardens, it rolled to a stop on top of the railroad tracks a few miles from work. Right dead center on top of the *working* railroad tracks.

I pushed it down into the parking space at the depot with one hand. A friend on her way to work saw me and gave me a lift to Busch Gardens and back home again. I didn't even lock it, and left the keys on the seat. No one stole it. *Quelle surprise.*

I told my sister she needed to get it fixed, because I was about done with it. She had it towed to a mechanic. The day it was ready – at the cost of another couple hundred bucks – she told me I had to pick it up. I got to the garage and was led to the back of the lot where they kept all the criminally shitty cars, and hopped in.

The stereo was missing.

I looked out at the mechanic and politely asked where the fuck the stereo was. He replied that he did not know. The foot long, drop-forged 1 and ½ inch open-end wrench in his hand suggested to me the conversation was over.

When I started the car up, it did not sound any better than when it went in. I putted out of the garage lot, using every damn swear word I knew, and creating a few more on the fly. I was still swearing ten minutes later on Highway 64, directly across from the Hampton Coliseum when Ralph died again.

It just stopped running, and rolled to a burial plot on

the side of the highway with an anti-climactic silence. I did not miss a beat: the second it stopped rolling I stepped out, left the door open, key in the ignition, and started walking the last six miles home. I don't even think I put it in park.

A nice man pulled over when I was more than three quarters of the way home and offered me a ride. I said no thanks, I needed to walk this one off. When I got home, I told my sister where she could find it, and I said I didn't want to ever hear about it again. I have no idea what ever became of it, and I don't care. The memories it brings back are too painful.

It would be a few years before I got a car all of my own. The '76 Mustang II Ghia I loved so much. You know, some people shit-talk Fords a lot, even make jokes about them that are hurtful. But all things totaled up equally, that car was still one of the best I ever owned, and that includes the blown out fuel filter I got on a country road somewhere between Cookeville and Crossville, Tennessee.

THEY AIN'T GONNA GET ANY DEADER

If you put the barrel of a gun to my head and demanded that I tell you honestly if I felt that I had ADHD or was somewhere on some Spectrum, two things would definitely happen. A) I would feel that this light chit-chat had escalated REALLY quickly for some random small talk at a party, and 2) I would slowly nod yes, yes I believe I am.

I have always had a bit of an awkward interpretation of life, and admittedly I truly believe this is mostly because of my early years of upbringing in the wild, and lack of travel and not being particularly well-read. But the other part is that I honestly feel there is some wiring thing going on. Maybe they used the last of those cloth-wrapped wires when creating me, so as to keep the cost down from not having to upgrade to the new plastic-coated wiring. Or perhaps they used that soy-based wire coating like Toyota did that one year, not realizing they were putting an all-you-can-eat rat and squirrel buffet under the hood.

Whatever the case, I am pretty slow on the uptake in general; and this fortunately and or unfortunately spills over into the fight/flight and understanding/empathization areas of my computing center.

I do not empathize well. I quite awkwardly have to force myself to do it most of the time, and I do not always interpret a "run-the-hell-away-NOW" message the right way or when I should. Sometimes this lack of "reading the signs" finds me face to face with a rather large hornet's nest, with a big container and a piece of plywood, feeling quite certain that I can "scoop that nest up in one go" and not have to kill the lot of them with napalm.

Sometimes it's also just me finding the dark, or maybe not-so-lightish humor in many situations that at first blush feel like they might possibly require a more somber demeanor. Death being one of them.

Now I do understand the somewhat finality of death, and what it does to those left standing around after someone else goes trotting off into it, but I have never really had the proper reaction to it. I tend to make remarks that do not always jibe with the sentiments of others in the room when the subject rears its ugly head.

I also know that there is a difference between 1) great grandpa dying at the age of 95 of death-related issues, and B) a best friend, spouse or child passing before their time, or quite young. There is a line I do not cross when I can help it because I understand the actual shittiness of this happening. And it should be noted that I do not make fun of *each and every dead person* I hear about.

I mean, I'm not a *monster*.

But... some tyrannical dictator dying, some unrepentant dirtbag getting some come-up in an odd way (or even an even way), a good dark joke – this shit is fair game.

- This just in: *Generalissimo Francisco Franco is still dead.*
- What's black and white and red and can't walk through revolving doors?
  A nun with a spear through her head.
- What was the last thing that went through Hitler's mind in the bunker at the end of WWII?
  A bullet. *

THAT shit still makes me laugh.

My wife has never agreed with me on this, this humor

---

* None of these are my own jokes, I have just always loved them.

at the expense of another human being, whether a real one, an imaginary one, or even a representative of a real type. We do not share *that* sense of humor.

"Don't speak ill of the dead," I am told quite a few times a month.

"But why?" I ask every time, knowing I shall be clouted with the Cudgel of Shame in each instance, decimated with logic about what speaking ill of the dead causes in scientific and spiritual terms.

"Why? They ain't gonna get any deader," I inductively reason.

"You just *shouldn't*. *reasons *reasons *reasons," I get back.

Honestly, I just do not *understand* why I shouldn't. Why ANYONE shouldn't. I honestly feel – or rather I *know* – beyond any doubt that not only are they, the subject of the deadness, truly NOT going to get any deader, but that also being dead does not absolve them of anything they may have done or not done while alive.

Being in a state of deadness does not make an asshole into a nice person all the sudden, deserving of hushed tones and reverence. An asshole that dies is now just a *dead asshole*.

Hypotheticals – the nun/spear-type of situations – are not only *not* real, but technically were not stated to actually *be* dead. I mean how does a dead nun, spear or no, walk through a revolving door under their own steam? She's clearly got someplace to be, or she wouldn't be wedged in that Theophilus Van Kannel-designed door frame to begin with. TOTALLY alive.

And frankly, fuck Hitler.

I also understand the right for anyone to have their own opinion about the subject as well. I know the way I react is not necessarily the norm, but I also know it is my right to do as I do. And in reality, this behavior is almost always kept to familiar company or like-minded friends and family.

Though, being not as perfect as I would like, I know sometimes it spills over, and I take the heat for it. And yet *still* I ask: *why should I not speak ill of the dead*? Why would it be all right for me to say Hitler is a huge prick nearly the entire time he is alive, but the *moment* he is declared dead, there should be an immediate shift in how we view him?

I don't get it. But that's me.

In fact, the only thing that even makes me balk for a nanosecond before I make some immensely comical quip about someone who has died, or any mention of impending death – is that I seem to have a penchant for killing people off. I don't know when it started, but there have been more than a few times where my merely *saying the words* appeared to have caused the action.

For instance: we were sitting at the table one day, a couple of us – I think my wife and kids, maybe my in-laws – not really talking about anything in particular. Somehow, the subject came up of US Presidents, some mild statements were made. I don't even recall the entire scope of the discussion, but apropos of some other statement that was made about President Ford, I said something akin to "Well that's probably what killed him."

BTW, in that moment, Ford was still very much alive and kicking as we sat at the table. Until less than an hour later when someone saw the news headline that Ford had just died, around the time I made that clever remark. Everybody looked at me. I had now killed ol' Gerald Ford. Just for a fair-to-middling joke opportunity.

Wasn't the first nor the last time that has happened either. Among the others I had snuffed out (Fidel Castro), was a friend of ours... Dr. Cloud, the consultant to the student newspaper my wife and I worked at in college.

We had not spoken with her in a while, when we got an email from her saying that she was just in San Antonio a day ago, and was sorry she did not have enough time to come see us in Austin.

Then we just sort of chatted back and forth a bit in that email thread. We found out that despite a serious issue – I think it was an aneurysm or stroke or some such she had in her brain – she was still touring quite a bit and speaking at colleges around the country. She just had to be careful because of her condition.

A little more backstory on Dr. Cloud and myself. She loved my wife – *absolutely loved her*. When my wife was editor of the student paper, she was a responsible adult. She knew how to navigate the waters not only of campus life, but also the labyrinth that was the administrative end of things – the department heads, the university president, Board of Regents et al. Dr. Cloud did not feel the same about me. Mostly, and fairly, because I was not medically capable of doing all that adulting.

And it's not even that she didn't like me. I found out much later that she really did, and we got along great AFTER I was no longer editor of the newspaper. I think she found me a guilty pleasure. She thought that I was funny in a way that she just could not appreciate in polite company. In short, I made her laugh an honest laugh.

So back to that email thread. Dr. Cloud and I had a last few emails together, during which we made remarks about her illness, to which she replied that she laughed. I asked her not to laugh too hard because I didn't want to be responsible for her death. We signed off, and then we never heard back from her.

My wife and I got a notice a few weeks later saying that Dr. Cloud had left us, right around the time of our last email together. The romantic in me wanted to believe I had something to do with it. Probably not; I mean, let's be real. But it was likely going to happen anyway, and I hoped it was just quick and painless due to laughing.

I believe the ability to make somewhat light of an existential trauma is not only what sets us apart from animals, but is also good for one's psyche. It helps one deal with a topic that is not easy to deal with.

My grandfather, on my dad's side, once told me, while standing at his wife's graveside:

"I'll be in there with her soon enough, Greg," he said.

Then paused so slightly before pointing to the ground

in front of the tombstone that also bore his name but no expiration date,

"Just remember to stick a straw in the ground for me so I can breathe."

Years later, when going to visit his and her grave, I had my brother stop at a florist around the corner. My brother looked at me "oh right, flowers" he stated.

"No," I said.

We walked in, I asked the florist if they had any straws, and got just as a weird a look from them as I got from my brother.

"No," they stated. Then they had a thought – "But what about this?" The florist grabbed one of these double-strength green tubes – the kind you would find in a bubble tea shop nowadays – but twice as long. These are used to help hold up larger, heavier flower stems, such as sunflowers.

"Soooo… you DO have straws, don't you, liar," I snarked in my head. "Oh, perfect!" I said out loud.

The florist made another weird face, matched by my brother, and gave me the straw for free.

When we got to the grave, I took out my knife, cut one end of the straw into a point and stuck it into the ground on my grandfather's side, and tapped it down into the turf with my knife handle.

I turned to my brother and his wife and told them what I promised Grandpa. They laughed "okay, okay."

I was sorry I wasn't there when he died; it happened

shortly after we moved to Austin. Not that it would have made a great deal of difference; he passed away on the floor of his bathroom one night. Incidentally, so did my mother's father, and if you don't think I have anxiety about THAT every time I set foot into the bathroom as I get older, you'd be SORELY mistaken.

I was sorry I did not get up there to visit the grave as often as maybe I should, and I was sorry I didn't spend more quality time with him while he was alive. I was also sorry it took so long to make good on the promise of installing a breathing straw for him.

But I knew one thing that was for sure: whether or not I even did *any* of that at all, it didn't change the way I felt about him... and it certainly did not make Grandpa get any more-or-less deader.

THAT
ONE
SUMMER

If we are lucky enough, we all have That One Summer.
You know the one: the one that movies get made about.
The one where class gets out on the last day of school,
and you and your friends embark on a hijinx-filled
summer romp, and seem to become adults all at once. Or
at the very least you have some adult situations that you
clumsily stumble through, figuring it out as you go along.
And if everything's all right, you enjoy every minute of
the stumble... if perhaps only in hindsight.

My summer was the summer of 1981, between my
Junior and Senior years in high school. A time spent
feeling almost like an adult... having a job working at
an amusement park, partying with friends, going to the
beach, making new friends from all over the state, falling
in love, and even seeing how life can change in the blink
of an eye. All with very little parental supervision.

That summer was consumed mostly by my job as a costume character at Busch Gardens. By day I'd run around the amusement park dressed as a rat, a beaver, a moose, a dragon, or a knight. My evenings were spent during the week with beer and pizza and movies. Weekends were parties, trips to Virginia Beach when doable, beer, epic arcade sessions, and the Rocky Horror Picture Show.

The park was open weekends during school, then when summer hit it was open all week. Being employees, we could go to the park for free whenever we wanted when we were off. Busch Gardens was one of those in-demand jobs for high schoolers, it beat flipping burgers, and it was just kind of fun. Even if you didn't have too many kids from your own high school working there, you made friends real easy and very fast.

Oddly enough, though, a lot of times we only knew first names there: Martin, Betty, Stu, Jennifer. To differentiate between two people who may have had the same first name, we called people by their first names and then what job they did; kind of like they did in the olden days, where Robert who made wagons soon became Robert Wainwright, and anyone who worked with metal became simply "Smith."

So in addition to the friends I already knew from school, I had friends like Bob Skyride, Heidi LeMans, and Allan Caricature. Bob ran the skyride that took folks for a birds-eye-view of the park on a 50-foot-high cable loop that stopped at each section. He had a dark brown Shawn Cassidy haircut, a class ring he loved to show off, and a very serious demeanor, though he could be rather fun.

Heidi worked at the Le Mans race track ride in "New France," where I worked. Blonde wavy hair, blue eyes, killer smile; she strapped kids into the little Model A-type old-timey cars that ran around a "race track" on a guide rail. I had a huge crush on her... as did almost every other young man who worked with her.

Allan was a caricature artist who worked in a little booth also in New France, drawing these giant-headed cartoons of park guests. He was a kind of tightly-wound/goofy kid with curly hair. On breaks sometimes I would stand around watching him draw, and pick up tips on making physical exaggerations work for you.

I used to hang out with these kids and a few others, plus two or three friends of mine from Tabb High, including Mike, who I car pooled with a lot, because we both lived in Bethel Manor.

Mind you, we were young drivers; I was 16, Mike may have been 17, which means between us, we had maybe two years worth of driving under our belts. And like young drivers – young male drivers – we made a LOT of bad decisions as they pertained to automobile handling. We drank and drove, we raced cars on the road, took the privilege for granted. But that changed over the course of two weeks' time that summer.

One night we both got off late, and left the park grounds around midnight on a Friday. I was driving us home, we were tired and we had had a beer or two in the parking lot. We were on Denbigh Boulevard, about half a mile before what we all called the "Car Catcher" – a huge, girthy oak about ten or twelve feet off the side of the road on the outside of a blind curve. It was coming up on our left; we never really thought much about it.

The road was pitch black, and we hadn't seen a car for quite a few minutes. All the sudden these headlights appeared in my rearview mirror, and they came up on our tail FAST. I had to shade my eyes from the glare. The car pulled past us on our left and just tore down the road toward the curve, all we saw were the tail lights; four big red plastic rectangles in a horizontal formation.

When the car jerked back into the right-hand lane, it overshot, swerved over onto the right shoulder, over-corrected again and pulled sharply to the left. Then we saw those horizontal tail lights go vertical as the car flipped to the left... but then stopped mid-flip. The red tail lights then bounced back to the right and became horizontal again.

"HOLY SHIT!" I remarked.

"What the FUUUUUCK?" agreed Mike.

We pull up closer, and we see the car, a big old four door sedan, now sitting on the grass next to the Car Catcher, its roof concave, front and rear windshields popped out, one body laying on the grass next to the car. Smoke and dust cleared as I put the car in park and we got out.

Another car came up slowly and we asked the driver to see if he could find a phone and call for help; he drove off after making sure we were okay.

When we got closer to the trashed car, we saw beer cans on the ground where the back door had opened and that passenger had crawled out and collapsed on the grass. The front windshield, lying on the hood, had a hole in it about the size of someone's forehead, and blood spattered on the spider-webbed cracks.

We didn't see any driver behind the wheel.

The guy on the ground got up slowly, we helped him sit against the car. The front seat passenger was out but breathing. By the time we heard the police siren, we noticed someone walking slowly toward the car from the field past the oak tree; when he got to us he just asked

"Are they okay?"

We didn't know, we asked him who he was... he said he was the driver (apparently he got out and ran immediately after the crash, then had a change of heart). Not a scratch on him. Cop pulled up, said emergency vehicles were on the way, and asked us who we were. We said we saw the whole thing, and told him what happened. The cop just shook his head like he'd seen this shit before. He took our information and said we should get home, we'd be hearing from them.

Sure enough, we were contacted about showing up in court a week or so later to testify about what we saw: the driver was going to jail for DUI and a few other related counts. Everybody in the car lived.

But the fun didn't stop there.

The morning we had to be in court, Mike was driving. We were going to court early, and we had to be at work later that same day. The courthouse we were going to was in an unfamiliar part of Newport News. The sun was still low enough that it was in our eyes as we cautiously drove, looking at street addresses.

At one intersection, I'm not sure if we missed the red light, or the car crossing in front of us ran his, but we T-boned his car GOOD. Fortunately, as we were not going very fast, all we did was total his car, insurance-wise.

The driver, a man maybe in his forties, got out slowly, and lumbered to the passenger side of his car, looked at it and just said,

"Damnit."

He looked over at us, he was tired, he had just come off a double shift. We could tell he was pissed, but he was too tired to kill us. A passing cop car stopped, took everyone's info, asked us what we were doing, we told him we were now late for court. He raised an eyebrow,

"So you're on your way to court to testify about a vehicle accident... and you just got in a vehicle accident?"

"Yes sir," Mike said, very respectfully.

The cop said he'd call in to explain what happened, and told us how to get there. We overheard the driver who got hit saying he had just made his last payment on his car the day before. We found out later he was at fault; he was tired and ran his light. No charges were filed.

Let me tell you, it took us a few weeks to even want to drive again. We car pooled with other friends; but when we started again, we drove like textbook new drivers... for a few weeks, anyway. Mike and I both agreed THAT shit was nuts.

Fortunately, us being young, those events didn't ruin our summer too much, it just maybe made us a tad more mindful when we drove. We felt a bit more inclined to stop at one or two beers when we had to drive, watched the lights a bit closer, stopped on yellows.

One night after work, Mike and I went to get a pizza and beer, and he asked if I had ever seen The Rocky Horror Picture Show. I told him how my sister and her boyfriend had tried to get us into it one late afternoon in Albany a few years earlier, but it was rated R and we couldn't get in. He smiled.

"Oh my God, man, you have got to see it," he laughed. "It's a total trip. People yell shit at the screen, they get up and dance, they bring squirt guns and toast..."

"What?" I was as confused as I was intrigued. Any movie where you could bring squirt guns and toast and yell at the screen, I was up for.

He looked at his watch and said we had missed the early showing, but that the midnight show was always better.

"Don't worry if you don't know the drill, you'll pick it up quick," he explained.

SOLD.

We went to the mall where it was playing and got our tickets early, because it always sold out early. We played

Asteroids and Galaga in the lobby until the midnight show opened, and I was hooked from the very first shout of

"LIIIIIIPPPPPSSSS!"

Mike was right. I may have slunk low in my seat that first night as he and everyone else in the theater did what you do in a Rocky Horror show, but by the second and third viewings, I was right up there jumping to the left, stepping to the right, running up and down the aisles with a newspaper over my head, and asking that age old question

"WHERE IS YOUR FUCKING NECK?!"

I have no idea how many times we saw that movie that summer, but I'd say if it was a few times a week every week, sometimes twice in row at the 10pm and Midnight shows, it was probably an understatement. Pizza... Beer... Rocky... Huh? was the standing game plan.

The only times we missed the show was when there was some other very worthwhile event happening that we were obligated to attend, such as Busch Garden Employee Nights, parties at friends' houses, or general teenage grab-assery where we could find it.

Employee nights at the park were fantastic; sometimes they'd have movies with drinks and food, but the best times were the "Open Park" nights. On these nights the park was open – all rides and games – for just us, no normies or whining park guests. They'd have a live band at the end of the night, usually some Punk-ish or New Wave group, and it just got wild. One of my favorite bands I saw there was this post punk group that was sort of a cross between Blondie and Plasmatics, who performed a lot of their own original music with quite off-color lyrics.

The great thing with the rides was that they took the brakes and governors off, so the rides went faster, and if you wanted – and the lines were short – the ride would just keep going. One night we rode the Loch Ness Monster roller coaster at top speed something like 6 times in a row without stopping. Ahhh, youth.

We'd be so wired by the time Management funneled us out into the parking lot, we'd make plans with coworkers on the spot to go do something else. And sometimes that something else involved trespassing on parkland that was closed, and running all over the grounds.

I have no idea how we ended up there that night, but Bob, Allan, Mike, Heidi and I found ourselves at the Mariners Museum grounds at 2am. The museum and grounds were closed of course, but *really* that was only for squares, not the type of go-getters who could jump the green iron fence around the park.

In the shadow of the giant ship's propeller set in a big stonework fence, I got my very first make-out session with Heidi. And yes, that'd be both the first one with Heidi, and the first one ever. We sat on a bench under a big oak tree, listening to Bob, Mike and Allan run around scaring each other in the dark. We were laughing, but we were also trying to figure out our next moves. It wasn't brain surgery, it happened whether we figured it out or not.

I can't say how Heidi felt about it – me being a 100% inexperienced 16-year-old, and she being a few years older – she may have been in college. But I knew how I felt about it.

"Yes, please."

We didn't get much more face-to-face time, as the three stooges we arrived with had gone silent, and yes, it was because they had learned to hunt together like velociraptors in the wild. They had noticed we were not among the loud, nitty gritty dirty little freaks running around trees just off Warwick Boulevard, and they decided to find us... quietly.

By the time Heidi and I had paused our face-squishing activities, and cocked our ears, listening for the kids like two parents who knew the significance of "no sound" in the other room, the unholy trio had popped up on three flanks, screaming like morons.

Sadly, for Bob at least, they caught us in a position that suggested Bob had lost his chance. Allan and Mike laughed, pardoned themselves, and told us to "carry on," quickly excusing themselves to go climb a tree. Bob paused a few seconds too long. I swear his lower lip was just about ready to jump off his mouth like a quivering blob of butt-hurt collagen, when Heidi jumped up, pulled me to my feet, and we chased after Mike and Allan.

AWWWWWWWK-ward.

You'll have to excuse me if I can't recall much else

from that particular night; everything after our lips first touched was a huge blur. Heidi and I had similar encounters once or twice before the summer was over, and I am pretty certain she was hoping for someone a little older, and a little more experienced than I was. But it was just as well, and it was all good; I thank her for her service.

The rest of my summer was pretty uneventful on the girlfriend – or even make-out partner – front. I had many more "no thanks you's" and missed opportunities from my inability to read the signs properly than I had actual Wins.

But it didn't matter; it was, I was to find out later, the last summer of its kind. Oh, I'm not saying I never had any more fun summers, filled with very few actual responsibilities; but the summers from then on were expected and copied experiences. THAT summer, that summer of '81... that was the *mold*. It was the Big Bang, the first for a lot of things... especially that *feeling*; that freedom, that precipice between being a kid and being an adult, where you learned about yourself and others. Any time after that when that *feeling* showed up again, it may have been fun, it may have been good or even great, but it was an echo of *that* summer, a derivative, a spin-off.

The original was in a class all its own... and it was going to be very hard to beat.

I
CAN
HOLD
MY
OWN
BEER

There is a saying, and it can come from any number of demographics, but typically you hear it from states such as Florida or Texas: "Hold my beer."

And the way you typically hear it is from a situation similar to this:

Two or more (typically) males (of any age) are watching a Thing happen. This Thing, whatever it is, is usually dangerous, and the unfolding of the tableau (to any normal person) is clearly not something anyone would want to do if they wanted to live another hour. One (typical) male will say to another,

"Man, that looks soooo dangerous. Ain't nobody could do that any more dangerouser than that. No sir, no how, no way."

To which one of the other males – and really, it is almost *always* that *one guy* – will say "HOLD MY BEER." At which point they will proceed to try to prove that nay-sayer incorrect. The ensuing actions will (if done right) result in a trip to the ER or the morgue.

The beer holding, while usually metaphorical in nature, can also be literal – as in a great deal of cases in Florida and Texas. But really, anywhere where males get together and watch dangerous Things in real life, and alcohol is a factor, you can get some spectacular results. Anything from "THAT WAS AWESOME!" or "What a DUMBASS," to the much less appealing, "CALL 911!"

I know this, because I am a male, I have been young, I used to drink a lot of beer... and also my Dangerometer is slightly mis-calibrated.

When I was in High School, in both New York and Virginia, I had a lot of friends who were country boys. One might even go so far as to mention the term Good Ol' Boys, or Rednecks.

In a Point of Clarification here, I must state for the record that I place no ill intent on the term "Redneck."

I mean, I know the connotation of the term, but the denotation is what I have no issue with. I considered myself a Redneck growing up. Folks with red necks got them by working hard outside in the sun for long hours, and the necks matched the "farmer tans" on their arms.

I'm just saying, in this scenario, the term brings up a type of person, and a lot of my friends *were* that.

The following two may not *necessarily* have been that. But they could DRINK.

I never went to school dances for the first two years of high school, anxiety I suppose. But one night, some of my wrestling friends convinced me to attend the Friday Dance; being cognizant of my feelings and any triggers they might accidentally trip, they cajoled me with,

"Stop being such a pussy, we'll pick you up at 7," said Rob.

"Yeah, Pussy," said Tom, "what are you going to do, be pussying around at home all night? Come on, it'll be fun. Pussy."

They certainly knew the value of a good burn, and they leaned into it.

At 7pm Rob and Tom picked me up in Rob's Gremlin, and we made a quick stop at the 7-11 around the corner for some Big Gulps.

I had been drinking for about a year now, which in semi-rural Virginia time was about 7 years. I could hold my beer, which I did a few times in the car to loosen up the death-grip my rectum had on the 2x4 it was holding. I knew how much my friends drank in theory... but I was about to see it happen in reality, and THAT, I was not ready for.

While driving, Rob asked me to "mix him a drink." He handed me his Big Gulp, told me to pour some out the window, and then to feel around under the seat, where I found a pint of Everclear.

For those of you who do not know what Everclear is, it is basically gasoline in a handy, ergonomically-designed bottle that is easier to use in a moving car than a typical pump nozzle. The only drawback is that there is no nozzle-lock with auto shut-off, so you have to do that manually when you dispense it into your mixer drink, in this case a Coke Big Gulp.

I poured a little Gulp out, added a little unleaded, stirred it with the straw, and went to hand it back to Rob. He side-eyed the hell out of the cup.

"Quit being such a pussy, man. Make me a *drink*." He said matter-of-factly.

I poured more out, added more Devil Liquid, he still shook his head. Let it suffice to say that when the final drink was done being mixed it was more Everclear than Coke.

"Ahhhh," he sighed after taking a long, loud slurp from the straw. "That's what I'm talkin' about."

I looked at Tom in the back seat, he shrugged, handed me his Big Gulp, and I made another one with the remains of what was in the bottle.

They offered me sips, I took a few for the Cool Points, but could barely hide the throat and facial spasms that resulted. Let's just say everyone in the car was warm and toasty when we arrived at the dance, me more than either of my friends who were quite used to drinking tractor fuel.

We parked in the lot next to the school, and were walking in on the sidewalk when we spotted Mr. T working the front door to the school.

"Shit." was the term that came from our mouths all at the same time.

Mr. Tylavsky was the Assistant Principal. He was a former Marine – he always made sure to say "Former," not "Ex" – who was definitely built like one. If ever you looked at a person and just *knew* from the way they carried themselves that they were BUILT under that suit and tie, and you did not mess with them – that was Mr. T. Also, he worked out in the gym with us wrestlers and football players, we knew he was ripped; we didn't let that shaggy black mane of thick hair and the giant Groucho mustache fool us. We got along okay, but we knew he'd rip us in half if we gave him half a reason.

"Okay," said Tom, "no big deal, just act normal, he'll let us in. Just be cool."

So we all shrugged our shoulders in preparation for coolness to settle into us, and we walked up to the door as cool as a polar bear sipping a milkshake on an ice floe off the coast of Svalbard.

"Gentlemen," barked Mr. T, "good to see you tonight." Then he looked all three of us in the eye at the same time for maybe two tenths of a second.

"You boys been drinking tonight?" he asked, as rhetorically as anything I had ever heard be rhetorical.

The three of us looked at him, looked at each other, palms up, shocked looks on our faces.

"What? No, Mr. T," Tom answered, "I just came from work."

"Yeah," I chimed in, "Rob just picked me up at home. This is my first dance." I smiled, now knowing fully well what I said, how I said it, and how the lobotomized grin on my face may have been dead giveaways as to our exact state of my inebriation.

Rob didn't say a word.

Mr. T looked us up and down, stared through our souls via our twinkling eyes. Time passed SOOOO slowly. Finally,

"Get inside, gentlemen, I do not want any trouble from you three tonight." He sighed, and opened the door for us.

Tom whispered sotto voce at us as we stepped one foot through the door.

"Told you, just be cool," he said.

"Nice," I said, scanning the open area. Then I double-taked across the commons to where I saw a girl I knew, who was a little nuts like me, and I had the biggest crush on her for a few years or so.

"HEY! A!" I shouted and threw my hands out to my sides, probably whacking Tom and Rob as I did so. "AAAAAAAAAA!" I shouted as I ran a few steps, dropped to my knees and slid the last 15 feet across the highly-buffed concrete floor to where Alis was sitting on a bench talking with some friends.

"What's up?!" I shouted as I came to a stop at her feet... *Cool. As. A. Fucking. Cucumber.*

Alis laughed.

Tom and Rob shook their heads as they walked normally into the school, trying to create some distance between me and them.

Mr. T had a vein popping in his forehead as he closed his eyes and turned his head for plausible deniability, and shut the door the rest of the way.

This story was just a primer. As you can see, no particularly dangerous stuff to deal with, other than the big mean Russian doorman. But things were not always so low key when hanging out with Rob and Tom and that damn Gremlin.

On any given night when we were hanging out at The Square – typically at the McDonald's, – it didn't take much asking to get at least one of us to do stupid shit with very little prep time. And it was often me that did some really stupid shit. And yes, there was definitely alcohol, and extremely possible that there was a girl somewhere in there fueling things along.

This one night, my memory fails me a bit on this one, but I want to say Rob was getting his Gremlin from where we parked. The rest of us were hanging out in the parking lot between Micky-Ds and Big Star, when an attractive female classmate and her friend showed up and were making small talk with us.

One thing led to another, like it do, and before long I was sitting on the hood of Rob's car, leaning against the windshield, hands in the air as he sped across the center of the parking lot.

"VVVVVVRRRRRRROOOOOOOOOMMMMM!" went the Gremlin

"WHOOOOOOOOOOOO," suggested I.

"SLOW DOWN DIPSHIT!" shouted some dick from another school who had NO idea what constituted fun on a Saturday night.

Rob cut hard to the right and slowed down. But here's the thing. I was not drinking *that* much before this, but there was still physics involved, and physics is the real culprit for most shit that happens to people, especially of a teen age.

We'd all be a lot happier and a lot less banged up were it not for "Sciencemath."

I never bothered with Physics in school; the furthest I made it in Math was Trig, and I had dropped out of that three weeks in. But I am certain the proof would be written something like this:

> *Car go fast in straight line.*
> *Object on car hood go fast in same direction.*
> *Car turn direction.*
> *Object on hood keep going same previous direction.*

Which I did.

I wobbled to an upright sitting position on the blacktop, dusted myself off, and checked for bone shards sticking through my clothing, but amazingly found there were none.

Another friend of mine ran up to me and laughed "HOLY SHIT, that was awesome!"

Apparently when I went whizzing off the hood of that car, I did a rather nice tuck-n-roll and landed on my ass, like I had planned it (I had not). Thank you wrestling training... all that tumbling/reflexes nonsense paid off in the self-preservation department.

Self-preservation went out the window at the end of that year, or rather at the end of the school year, anyway. Shortly after graduation, the famed Gremlin met its Maker at an intersection not a mile from the school.

I was staying at Mark's house for the summer, and he picked me up at the ER. We picked up my pain meds from the pharmacy, went home, and I took a nap. When I got up, we went to a party, where we had a nice assortment of drinks that included many beers.

When we left the party, Mark and I went by the Ol' Square to see who was still hanging out, and we of course met some girls from another high school. I was sitting in the back seat with one girl, Mark was driving with the other girl up front, and as is mandatory, we started doing donuts in the parking lot.

I of course was laughing in the back seat with the nice young lady as we spun in a clockwise direction, and everything was fine... until the car went counter clockwise. I grabbed the Oh Shit Handle above the window to stabilize myself, but a speed bump sent me into the window. My injured elbow whacked it pretty hard and blood splattered on the glass.

Then the screaming started.

First by the girl sitting with me, who I'll just bet thought I cracked my head open. Then her friend turned around to see what was the matter, and she started screaming. Then Mark turned around.

"SHIT," he said. And the car came to a stop, the girls got out and ran, Mark and I looked at my bleeding elbow.

"I think I popped my stitches," I said.

We looked at the blood on the window. Time to go home.

I forget where I was going with this story, but bottom line, kids: *please drink responsibly*.

THIS
IS
WHY
I
CAN'T
HAVE
NICE
JOBS

Yeah, I grew up on a farm. It wasn't a big farm, like where you raise animals, combine the corn, and grow enough vegetables to be sold by the metric ton at the market at the end of the year. It was what is known as a subsistence farm, meaning that we grew enough for ourselves, and sold whatever overflow we had at a folding table on the side of the road at the end of our driveway.

Needless to say, this practice was work, but it was not by any means what I would have called "my first job." I mean most people consider their first job to be some sort of professional thing where One wears a suit and tie, and answers phones like,

"Good Afternoon, thank you for calling Wambaugh, Spaciturn & Devereaux, how may I help you?"

Which would be followed quickly by something like

"Thank you, will you please hold one moment while I connect you to Ms. Spaciturn's office?"

Nobody in the office, especially the younger schmucks like you – who are still in high school – knew exactly what it was that Wambaugh, Spaciturn, or Devereaux did, made, or offered, but by God... those numbers better be up by the end of the week or somebody will be scanning the Want Ads for a new job by EOD Friday.

Wambaugh, what a bully. Always threatening folks with their jobs.

It could be said that my first pay-checked job was working in a brewery in the French Quarter of a multi-cultural community. But it would be more correct to say that I was a costume character rat at Busch Gardens: *The Old Country* in Virginia the summer after my Junior year of high school.

Busch Gardens, the theme park that was adjacent to the brewery in Williamsburg, was a short drive from our school, so a lot of us worked there. Some friends told me about it, and then my theater friends informed me of the fine opportunities in Live Entertainment: musical shows, plays, little side shows that wandered the park or worked out of fun little wagons fixed in an area. Live E, as it was called, also paid 25 cents an hour more than the "regular" bullshit jobs of ticket-taking, sweeping, food sales, etc.

We made $2.75 per hour. And when we, as high school students, got that first $125.00 check for a standard work-week (with OT), it was bedlam. The pizza, the beer, the movies, the filling up of the gas tank and the driving around, the albums, the miscellaneous. I had never seen so much (steady) money in my life.

The job-getting process was a bit of a learning curve for me, because I had no experience in applying for jobs. I had no resume to speak of, which would have hindered me at almost any other job.

But for this one, all I needed was light background on myself, and some well-fudged items from school like plays I had been in, sportsy mentions to show athleticism, and a picture of myself. That all got me in the door for my interview, which was really an audition. My first ever *professional* audition, as a matter of fact.

A friend of mine and I drove in, he had an interview for a Normie job, and I went over to the "Globe Theatre" in Banbury Cross, the English-themed section of the park. It was a weird-ish experience, because the empty park felt very apocalypse-like, too quiet. But it also smelled of hops and brewing, it was like breathing in a case of beer, which was not bad, really, for a teenage boy.

During the months when the park was in full swing, you really didn't smell the hops much; they were drowned out by the scent of the sea of humanity, the food, the smells of machines, oil, water, some animals, etc.

In my audition, we hopefuls all sat in the Globe's audience seating and watched each before us go up on stage and get some light direction from the Grand Pooh-Bah there, who watched us perform one of three different improv scenarios.

I remember later realizing, once we were working together, that I had seen two guys who became good friends perform the same scene prompt I was given, which was:

> *"You're a chair. You watch a very cute*
> *girl come into the room, and she needs a*
> *place to sit, you try to get her to sit on you.*
> *Then she does. Then she leaves. And then*
> *a really fat girl comes in and wants to sit*
> *on you."*

That may not be exactly word for word... but it's pretty darn close. Wow. WOW.

I was a teenager; what did I know. I was a teenage boy; what did I care. I did the thing, watched as Mr. Pooh-Bah with his starched chambray button-down shirt, salmon-colored sweater draped over his shoulders, and khaki shorts that matched his docksiders sat there with a chuckle escaping in spurts from under his thick, cheesy pornstache. Did I mention I did not care much for Mr. Pooh-Bah? There was something I really just did not like about him AT ALL.

We were all thanked for our service, told we would be contacted, and released from the realm. A few days later I got the call that I had been hired; I would be playing the character of Rufus the Rat in the New France section of the park. YAY! I was employed!

With great appreciation and enthusiasm, I went in for my costume fitting, got my Dress Whites that we wore under the costume (really just white boxer shorts, T-shirt and socks... underwear), and Chaperone Outfit (some buckskin-mimicking get-up). Then I was shown the trailer where I'd be working, filled out paperwork, was told how happy they were that I was now part of the Live E family and blah blah blah.

Aaaaaannnndddd that was pretty much the last time I really got any contact with the powers that be.

Opening day (for me, anyway), the newbies showed up to meet the other few established employees, and we were suited up and released into the park, basically getting hands-on training in the moment. Two of the new costumers were those two I mentioned: Nic who played Buford the Beaver, and Mike who played Mortimer the Moose. We still talk to this day, diverse and different as our lives have gotten.

The other three were Jenny, Henrika, and Millie, who would be playing Pierre the Mouse, Bevo the Fox, and Tallulah The Toad. None of us knew dick about being costume characters. Everything was brand new, and we wanted to do good at our jobs, which, by the way, were *quite* fun.

That all spiraled down into a maelstrom of typical unchaperoned teen male behavior rather quickly.

Don't get me wrong, we had a few good weeks of getting to know the ropes, we all bonded as much as we needed to, and we were all having a pretty good time. We learned we could head out into the park and have fun in between "shows," meeting the other employees in our section and others.

We figured out quickly how to make friends with the folks who worked the concession stands so that we could get even bigger discounts and free food later.

One of the tastiest treats in the park was this multi-layer Black Forest chocolate cake that they served in the German section. Trays of it were sent to other areas of the park as well. It was a pride thing that these slices of cake were served standing tall: all the layers of rich chocolate cake, and creamy filling, and whipped cream and cherries were all visible in an upright form.

If the cake slices ever fell over, they were removed from the case up front, and the fallen angels were set in the back, where us riff-raff employees could get them for free before they were thrown away.

If there were no available rejects, and a friendly server wasn't available to "accidentally" topple one for us, we learned how to reach around the serving window and make one go down. My favorite lunch was the fried chicken, grape soda, and toppled Black Forest cake served at the Mackinak Cafe. SOOOO Canadian.

Blind ambition, or perhaps boredom more likely, got us all switching costumes, and by the end of the summer we each had played all the characters in our trailer. Some of us even got the chance to go TDY (Temporary Duty) to other sections of the park and play those Costumed Characters – including getting to be the Park Mascots, St. George and Gordon the Dragon. Those two were coveted spots, as they got the most pictures taken with them. Gordon because he was such a cute, cuddly (80-pound) vinyl dragon; St. George because you could actually see his face, and that suit of armor was a glistening chic-magnet.

But in our assigned sections – we covered France and New France (Canadia) – it was Rufus, Buford, Tallulah, Bevo, Mortimer, and Pierre. Why they felt they needed both a Rat and a Mouse was beyond me; I guess France was known for plague-ridden rodentia.

The shortest of us was the girl who played Pierre, Jenny. She was maybe 5 feet tall; the tallest was Mike, who was six foot something or other... and yes, it was hilarious (to us) to watch the short folks swap costumes with the tall folks, and see the leggings ride up over the calves, or bunch up around the ankles.

It was also a lot of fun when the Normies out in the park, the public, had some dude-bros (not called that at the time) who thought it was funny to try to molest the "obviously" female characters, only to find out it was one of us lads instead. I do recall a very quick shoving-fight or two with some jerks. I like to think in our own way, we gave the punks out there pause in thought when thinking they could be gropers.

One of our favorite gags in costume was figuring out

how to grab snacks and drinks from the ice/snack carts that were pushed around the park. We'd do these little "bits" where the costume character would pretend to be overcome by the heat, then they'd run over to the snack cart and start to thrash around in the ice to the amusement of both the public and the cart operator. What we were really doing was stuffing snacks and treats under our oversized heads or into our suits, to be enjoyed later in our trailer.

Sometimes we'd borrow a little stuffed animal from the pile of prizes at one of the game stalls, and then go find a girl or boy we thought was cute, and tell them they'd won a prize for being the Best Looking Guest of the Day, and we'd take our picture with them. Sometimes we got phone numbers, sometimes we got caught by the Game Stall folks, most of whom had very little sense of humor as it pertained to end-of-day inventory counts.

It was late in the summer when our off-brand shennaniganian activities caught the attention of our new immediate supervisor, who – with *much* hoit and toit – was too busy only hanging out with the live stage performers in the theaters around the park to pay us costumed characters much attention. Oh dear God, do NOT leave Greg unattended when he feels like no one gives a flying care about what is going on.

We'd get a call on The Phone, a black dial phone set on the wall of the trailer. It was only used to communicate with the office if we had an emergency, or for them to call us for any reason, such as complaints from "Secret Shoppers" – shills from the office who would roam the park making sure everything was hunky-dory.

Turns out they did not think everything was hunky-dory in New France.

Our new immediate supe was a bitchy, humorless ladder-climber who did not like the boss Mr. Pooh-Bah any more than I did. She wanted his job. And you know who she hated more than him? Yes. It was me.

Hi, I was the problem, it was me.

I don't even remember her name, but I did not care for her one teensy bit. Her just-ate-a-raw-lemon look that was always on her face, that screechy knife-grinder voice, and that pompous, arrogant attitude that you could feel just *wafting* across the ground as she approached in her heels, like a toxic gas-leak from a ruptured Soviet chemical plant.

Well, Gas Leak decided to make me her pet project, and unfortunately, I was only too happy to provide her with all the foamboard, glue, noodles, and glitter she needed for that project. Sometimes we knew when she was coming; the park had eyes and ears. Other times, we got news that Admin was away from the park that day, and things got TURNT.

But ultimately, the cards were stacked against me – and I pretty much did that shuffling myself, I know that. I got busted, and I deserved it, mostly. Kinda.

Gas Leak was able to finally shove Mr. Pooh-Bah into a meat grinder, and did indeed take his spot as Director of Live E. What I didn't know was that Pooh-Bah really liked all of us, and always had our backs, which is why we had gotten away with so much shit up to then. That changed on a dime.

I was given the "I've got my EYE on you" talk in short order, and told if I got caught being anything other than a *model employee* of Anheuser-Busch International, Inc., its partner United Parks & Resorts and its subsidiary Busch Gardens: The Old Country, I would be drummed out of the corp.

Understood. You didn't have to tell ME something twice. Got it. Keep my nose clean. *Which* I was able to do. For a very short amount of time. Like, I think it was the remainder of that day.

Upon further consideration, it was determined that I did not care for the *tone* with which I was spoken to.

The next day, when I thought Gas Leak was out of the park, I engaged in one of my favorite pasttimes: in my dress whites, I sat on the old weathered wooden wagon (it was set dressing) between our trailer and the open park, and smoked some clove cigarettes. The clove cigarettes were an affectation I'd picked up from some older kids at a party one night. I thought they smelled great, and made you more than *ironiquement sophistiqué*.

I'd just sit there, very continental like, my legs crossed, arms folded until I needed to puff smoke out, and wave at the train cars that took guests around the entire circumference of the park. This train went by maybe fifteen feet from that wagon, where I sat on an old crate or barrel, basically smoking in my underwear and work boots.

The phone call came rather quickly. Gas Leak invited me to take the rest of the day off, and then come see her first thing the next morning. Okay. Not my first rodeo on being called into the Principal's Office; but I truly felt that I had done nothing wrong that day. So if I was to get sacked, I might as well go out in style.

I donned my Rufus the Rat costume in the mirror one last time, in a smash-cut montage like you see in the movies. The famous riff from Muddy Waters' *Mannish Boy* played over it in my head:

* Bulk of the body suit shrugged over my shoulders

Bah DAH DAH dah DUMM

* Zipper zipped up to the base of my skull

Bah DAH DAH dah DUMM

* Left paw oooooon

Bah DAH DAH dah DUMM

* Right paw oooooon

Bah DAH DAH dah DUMM

* Head on, chin strap in place

Bah DAH DAH dah DUMM

* Trailer door kicked open from inside

*SKKKREEEEEEE-OOOOOOOOOOOOOOO**

I imagined a slow-clap from my compatriots as I strutted out the door, and down the back lot, past the Country Show, past the Mackinak Cafe and those delicious Black Forest cakes. Stephanie, a cute street sweeper I knew, saw the Dead Rat Walking, and stopped

---

*"SKKKREEEEEEE-OOOOOOOOOOOOOOO" is copyright 1982, George Thorogood.

sweeping up snack wrappers and cotton candy cones long enough to shout after me, one defiant fist raised to the sky, a tear in her eye,

"WAY TO GO RUFUS... *sobs quietly*... way to go...!"

I snapped a salty salute to her as I marched straight across the blacktopped ground to the long concrete ramp down to the queue for the Log Flume ride. Guide ropes ignored with much sass, I Slapped Five to kids as I made my way to the front of the line. A summer-long dream of mine was about to reach fruition. The perfect melding of my favorite character meeting my favorite ride in the park.

Which also happened to be a *very* strict taboo for us Costumers.

The park visitors LOVED riding with me as we hit the smaller drops on the way to the top of the Big Drop. We all raised our hands over our heads as we plunged down the gorge, water splashing us all till we were soaked. We exited to the right of the ride when we were done. I shook hands and posed for pictures as I walked with families and couples back up to New France Proper.

I was a Golden God.

And the next morning, I went in to take my licks.

My 16-year-old-this-is-the-first-real-paycheck-job-I-ever-had ass sat across the desk from Gas Leak, who could barely contain her joy at being able to fire me. So naive, I still believed that when people asked a question, they wanted a real and truthful answer to it.

Questions like:

"Are you okay, Greg, has anything been bothering you? How can we help you have a better experience here at Busch Gardens?" Gas Leak asked with a look of the sincerest sincerity anyone could ever sincerely muster – a look I have since learned was pure BS, and the bright, loving eyes were really just the dead shark-eyes of a predator enjoying the scent of blood in the water.

"Well," I started, then cleared my throat, gathering my nerve, and a bit excited that this boss actually wanted to hear what was bothering me so that she could help.

"I have noticed that you don't seem to care much about us down here in the Costume Character department, all your time is spent up in the..."

I did not get to finish my sentence. I did not get to say almost anything, as a matter of fact. Gas Leak asked if there was anything I wanted to cop to, like maybe something untoward, slightly unseemly, and w*aaayyy* against Park Policy I may have done recently, such as, saaaaayyyyy YESTERDAY AFTERNOON?

With pursed lips, and eyelids pulled up or down as far as they would go, I looked over at the fake plant in the corner of the office and tried to think of *anything* that came to mind.

"Nnnn..."

"DON'T. EVEN. TRY. LYING." She blasted in her infuriatingly high-pitched spoiled princess brat voice.

From thence on, for the next two minutes and twenty-three seconds, Gas Leak informed me that she was mortified – *mortified unto death* to hear that – when her boss, The Suit*, was riding the train around the park, she saw a young man, *in his underwear, smoking cigarettes* on the wagon in the New France Section of the park.

She was beyond SHOCKED as this young man actually had the audacity to wave at her as he blew smoke. And – and this is the part that truly Strawed the Camel – it wouldn't have been so bad if it were just The Suit on that train (like she needed any further excuse), but it just so happened that day was the day The Suit was showing some dignitaries from Japan around the park. And *they* had questions.

I may have been young and inexperienced, but even I knew it was futile trying to lie. I mean, I tried anyway, but Gas Leak was pretty damn certain it was me. Just as certain as she was that THIS was also me:

She then slapped a glossy 8x10 photo of Rufus riding the Log Flume ride as it hit the Big Drop... staring directly at the Souvenir Photo camera as it strobed to capture the moment.

The sudden, half-swallowed guffaw that erupted from all the holes in my face is what I will presume slipped the last nail into my overly-fastened coffin lid. My fate was sealed, and I was on my way to a pattern of behavior that led me to where I am today, which is to say unemployed with only myself to blame.

---

*The Suit was what we called Gas Leak's boss, the operational head of Live E. I had nothing against her; she was just a company person that had to toe the line.

But at least now I can typically beat The Suits to the punch if I so desire; knowing when to self-eliminate, and when to stick around until they trebuchet my ass over the walls and out of the Kingdom.

My time at Busch Gardens was some of the happiest I had as a young man, so much so that the next year I got hired by the company that did the custodial work for the whole park, just so that I could still get in for free, see my friends, ride the rides and play the games whenever I wanted.

The privilege was paid for with emptying hundreds of trash cans, sweeping, mopping, and wiping down tables and chairs in gigantic special event buildings and restaurants, not to mention cleaning about 700 toilets every night.

Seven hundred toilets in an AMUSEMENT PARK.

An amusement park that served fried chicken, hamburgers, corn on the cob, cotton candy, seven-layered Black Forest cake, sticky, sloppy, foamy sugar-and-dye-based drinks, and, more importantly, BEER.

These treats were consumed by people from all over the world who would then ride rides and walk around in the sun almost assuredly not drinking enough water. Many of these customers barely made it to the bathroom in time. Some of the bathroom stalls needed to be locked from the inside and then army-man-crawled out from under, or over-the-topped, they were so bad. A few days later, when dried, they could be chiseled clean and then cloroxed.

In basically 12 months' time I learned everything I needed to know about being employed for the rest of my life. There are fun jobs, and there are hard jobs, there are good bosses and bad bosses, but it all comes down to *you* as to how you deal with them. Regardless of what *the work* is, sometimes putting up with other people's shit is the job you are *actually* getting paid to do.

HOW'S THAT WORKING OUT FOR YOU?

If you're anything like me, you've sat there, at least once or twice by the age of 50, looking at yourself in the mirror, and asking,

"What the hell have I done with the past twenty years of my life?"

Maybe also,

"Where the hell did the last 30 years of my life go?"

And perhaps even,

"I should definitely NOT have used that in-home hair dye kit, I look absolutely ridiculous."

I think I can safely surmise that most people over a certain age have taken even a fleeting glance backward in wonder and/or amazement as to how and why they are where they are today. And I'll bet almost none of them are particularly happy with the way things turned out on some level.

The plans we had when we were young and awesome – as we stepped out into the real world for the first time after high school; the boldness and determination with which we strutted away from college, certain that we would just take the world by storm – just never seemed to happen for a great many of us.

I know many of us feel this way, and almost always feel that this is a bad thing – this "not having things work out the way we planned, or hoped, or dreamed."

But just chillax, it ain't *always* a bad thing, even if it feels like it. A lot of times, we don't even really know for sure where those tangential lives started, where our original plans diverged into what we are now. So just take it easy on yourself.

Me, I know exactly when and where my life took its first, major BIG left-hand turn away from what I thought I wanted more than anything. I had the luxury of knowing, and with that knowledge I was able to sit back and think about what might have been, and realize it would NOT have gone well.

Now, I have said before that I did not have a great deal of self-confidence when I was younger, and had more than one person's share of anxiety. But there was one thing that I just never doubted about myself, and that was my ability to *nail it* when it came to performing in front of an audience; especially for laughs, and almost always regardless of the consequences.

When I was fresh out of high school, at the end of the summer after graduation, my friend Mark and I spent a particularly debauched week at UVA in Charlottesville, VA. We stayed with another friend, who had graduated the year before us, in his condo near campus. We lied or fake ID'd ourselves into the various clubs and venues that were sprinkled liberally around campus.

On the second floor of some coffee house or other, there was this music den, a cozy fireplace-and-couch type room, sat 50-75 I guess. I was sitting on the arm of a comfy broken-in sofa, chatting up some young ladies, having a few St. Pauli Girls' worth of liquid encouragement.

One of the girls, who I am thinking did not care much for me, certainly was not laughing at my antics as much as her friends, and was only trying to be a good Wing Woman for her girlfriend, said I was "drunk, underage, and probably needed to just go home." For the record, she was not wrong on any of those counts.

"Challenge Accepted," said my brain, naturally comedic instincts, and whatever ego I had at the time. I was going to get her to laugh as well, because nobody, *nobody*, was going to not at least giggle when I was in full swing.

"Drunk? DRUNK? Don't make me LAUGH!" I said, and I threw my head back and laughed a pretty exaggerated, ridiculous laugh; which threw me off balance, making me topple over backwards, feet flying up in the air, and head barely missing the stone hearth directly behind me.

The two fun girls chimed in unison "OH MY GOD!" The stern friend screamed, thinking I had fallen into the fireplace.

I found my bearings, got to my feet, noticed I still had some beer in my glass, downed the rest of it, and then struck the internationally recognized and sanctioned "TA-DAAAAAH" pose.

The girls had all left, there were a few stares from other patrons of the bar, stares accompanied by the sad head shake that One gets when they realize *somebody* is underage and does not know dick about how to comport Oneself in the Upper Society of a college dive bar.

That was me at 17.

Anything for a laugh, damn the torpedoes.

The reason we were in this college space to begin with, was because Mark and I were having a fun summer-after-graduation-romp before we set off to be the Next Big Things in Hollywood.

Mark was a pretty good friend for the last two years of high school, we hung out a lot, and in fact I lived with him and his family for the past six months or so, as my Mom had moved to Nevada where her husband had been re-stationed at Nellis Air Force Base.

This was a thing that happened with a lot of families that were military. The kid's – Military Brats, as they were called – parent(s) would get re-stationed somewhere, but the kid might be a Senior and wanted to stay and finish High School with their class. So, I stayed with Mark.

I was active in theater somewhat, and he had started to get into it as well. We did a few experimental-ish short plays together, one of which was Woody Allen's *Death Knocks*. Mark had a friend already living out in San Diego who was working in the entertainment field, and we were going to go stay with him until we got famous – under two months *tops*, we calculated.

So plans were made and tweaked and scheduled and honed for some time. We had it all down to one backpack and one steamer trunk each.

At the end of summer, Mark and I packed those black, silver-clasped trunks with as much as we could, jammed them into the trunk of the Mustang I had inherited when my mom and stepfather left, then my sister and her boyfriend drove us to UVA and dropped us off. The car was technically *half* hers, and from then on became *all* hers, as I didn't feel that argument was worth the trouble or brain cells.

So there we were, partying and drinking, drinking and eating, having a fantastic send-off for ourselves, talking about nothing but Hollywood and the start of our new lives.

The night we were supposed to leave Virginia, the train departed the station at like 11pm or some such; Mark took off with our UVA friend to go do something, leaving me to fend for myself for dinner.

I fired up the hibachi out on the balcony, grabbed whatever beer was left, and had myself a ribs-and-St-Pauli-Girl picnic. When they showed back up a few hours later, I was singing along to Simon and Garfunkle's *Kodachrome* at the top of my lungs, and chucking rib bones and empty St. Pauli Girl bottles over the balcony into the bushes.

You know, college man stuff.

The time came, we put our trunks into our friend's car, got driven to the station, and checked the schedule one last time. Mark went and checked the trunks in, I went to find the train. Mark and our friend came back just as the train was boarding. I eagerly jumped up on the train car's steps, and turned around to say one last Thank You and Take It Easy to our friend. Mark had one foot hovering over the bottom step in preparation to board the already chugging train...

Then he pulled his foot away... took two steps back.

"I can't," he said.

I just stared at him. Then looked at our friend. But there was no sign of anything there. Then back at Mark.

The train started moving.

"Okay, man. Take it easy." Was all I could say.

I turned and went into the train car, found my seat by a window, and watched, with SO many thoughts, as the train built up speed. Mark and our friend played out a ridiculous version of the "Train Goodbye Run" you see in the movies outside my window. I laughed; it *was* pretty funny.

I spent the next two days thinking about nothing else except California. Then the eventual dread that built up inside me won out by the time I got to Las Vegas, where we had planned a short stop to recoup and bathe and eat real food again before the last leg to Los Angeles on the Desert Wind.

I am not entirely sure if it was critical thinking, or just the crippling anxiety and depression that made the decision, but I never got back on the train. I stayed in Vegas.

In due course, I found an acting "agent," started doing stand-up, and enrolled at UNLV as "something to do" during the day to pass the time before my open mic gigs at night.

Years later – *decades* later – I reconnected with Mark via the technical wonder that is social media. One of the first things out of his mouth was a pretty sincere apology about the whole debacle. I really did not even plan on talking about it, and honestly had not thought about it in quite a few years. You know, despite the first ten years after it happened, in which I plotted several intricate revenge scenarios where he died a horrible death in each, missing different body parts each time. I laughed, thanked him, told him it was totally unnecessary.

"Man, we were kids. Dumb kids with stupid dreams." I said. "Besides, I wouldn't have the life I have today if I had gone to California. No harm, no foul."

I didn't harbor any ill will toward him at all: he made the right choice for him. I really love the story, though; I retell it a few times here and there, mostly as a way of getting my kids, or any other young person, to cut themselves some slack when it comes to "I shoulda this, or shoulda that."

I had come to know in the ensuing decades since that three-day train ride, that I would have been chewed up and spit out with great prejudice had I gone to California, very specifically to be a "Star," at that age and level of maturity. I know it.

In the much smaller industry market I wound up living and working in, I experienced it daily. I would *not* have handled the milieu well. I have seen other friends and acquaintances try it, and almost to a person, it did not work out well and they moved back a short time later – and they were all very talented, highly-motivated people.

It is a tough life, in a tough city, in a tough industry. What it IS, and what you end up PAYING for it, for what it DOES for the world – in my opinion – is not something that was worth it for me.

I dodged a bullet.

YOU
ARE
HERE

It's weird when you stop and think about where you are in the Whole Scheme of Things. Not even as in "how you fit into the world," necessarily, but rather, where you actually are in the timeline of humans, where you are in the timeline of your family, and how you may check out, and who will follow you.

This typically happens when I have some free time on my hands. Like between jobs, or when I am supposed to be working on something important, and maybe even a few times when my wife is asking me what I think of this new paint sample for the bedroom.

It sounds stupid and unimportant – *but when you stop to think about it* – it is not very trivial at all.

Let's say we are talking about a timeline, with left-to-right readability, wherein the left represents time before you, and let's say a green dot represents the time of your birth, and to the right of that Green Dot represents time after you showed up. The left-hand side, as one might imagine, goes on forever, for like three hundred forty-eight miles; and the right-hand side has a Big Black Dot maybe half an inch or less to the right from where you first show up.

And that Big Black Dot... means YA DONE.

On the left of your Green Dot, very close to your Green Dot are your siblings and parents and grandparents, maybe you were lucky enough to know your great grandparents. In today's world you may have even snooped around online and found some fifth-great-grandmother with a weird sounding name from a foreign country, such as Zuzanna Babesch, who was born in Finland but grew up in Austria, and died three years before the first Pilgrims were being eaten by Croatoanian demons in Roanoke, Virginia.

You know how they used to do those blood tests when people got married to make sure "they weren't already related?" It was a futile gesture. We are all related and inbred going back millennia. No wonder we are so messed up as a race.

Makes me actually laugh when someone asks me if I "Did the Ancestry DNA test yet!?" I always say the same thing:

"I can tell you what it's going to be: 38% X, 12% Y, 3% Z, and then a little bit of literally everything else out there. Because that is exactly what we all are."

Back on your timeline, you then see a few splinter-families and distant cousins going farther left, but they all petered out because writing, and language, and paper and ink etc. But you know – you JUST KNOW – that way farther back, before Plymouth Rock, before Charlemagne, before King Tut... we ALL have a Great Grandma Chargk and a Great Grandpa Glonk.

Now I know some of you are out there saying,

"Nuh-UHHH, Adam and Eve are everyone's grandparents from 9 thousand years ago. Nice Try."

Well, here's the problem with that, and I know the rest of you are already seeing this. If we start with Adam and Eve, we get to the same place, except the toothless banjo-pickers show up in the family tree almost immediately. Nine thousand years simply is not enough time to get rid of the stink that would have had to happen in order for humankind to spring from just two people.

Soooooooooo

Chargk and Glonk lived on the lower east side, not of any city, but the lower east side of the continent Pangea. Glonk was an intolerant bigot who really talked bad about the Neanderthals.

"No daughter of mine is going to marry some four-foot-two rock-banger," Glonk would grunt. "We walk up-right... erect, one might say. We can make the burning flower, and we eat meat that we have burned over said flower. Just look at the dwelling we huddle in when the sky makes angry noise and wets the dirt!"

And he would gesture toward the state-of-the-art

(crude) grass hut he thatched together in a hurry a week ago.

Chargk rolled her eyes for the umpteenth time, because she has heard this all before. Of course, she knew Glonk could be tad judgmental of the Neanderthal people as a whole, and yes, he had on occasion joined in with the hunting parties that wiped out entire caves-worth of them.

But Chargk was pragmatic, and had patience, she knew they could work together, and indeed live together in peace. She was all-in on their daughter's (your 140,000-great grandmother's) fast-approaching nuptials to Flarth, a nice young rock-bang... uh, Neanderthal from that cave three-suns-walk away.

"Don't talk like that in front of our daughter," grunted Chargk. "He's a nice boy, and he's very clever. You want to start talking bad about people... I think we all remember *your* mother when you first dragged me by the hair into your home..." and then she bent her knees and started to waddle around the grass hut while she slapped her palms on top of her head, and coughed out "ooh ooh oohs." This action of course got the dander up on ol' Glonk.

"MY MOTHER HAD A MEDICAL CONDITION!" he snorted, "why are you ALWAYS bringing that up?!" and the two wound up fighting like they always did. Chargk whacked Glonk with her plant-mashing branch, and Glonk took a swipe at Chargk with his weird-ass animal jawbone that seemed like it was just *glued* to his hand all the time.

Their daughter, Schnord, and her beau Flarth just

stood there witnessing this spectacle. Schnord, *completely* embarrassed by her father's behavior, and Flarth wondered what the hell he'd gotten himself into. It was a lot of fun making out behind the mastodon carcass in the field that couple of times, but this... *this* seemed to be getting out of hand rather quickly.

Poor old Flarth, he was in a bit of a rock/hard place situation. He knew his people were dying off, and his only chance of passing on his genes was to marry one of these ugly, straight-walkers, with their high-falutin' foot-skins, and literal home-made homes, and spoken words, and whatnot. This was Go Time for the Neanderthal, even if they couldn't find the words to say it... and trust me, they had searched all 37 of their "spoken" (grunted) words.

As expected, Glonk eventually drank some Gray Berry Ale and grudgingly attended the wedding ceremony. After which, they all went over to Flarth's cave and had their official family portrait done on the south wall, in that cavern where the temperature never seemed to changed, right next to "Big Animal Hunt with Pointed Sticks (red berry juice, hand, on granite)," that Flarth's brother had done. They all stuck their hands in some red goo, pressed their palms on the cool stone, and your family tree got another branch. A branch that mattered.

This is to say nothing of those that came even before Flarth's side of the family. At some stage in the Timeline of Life, there was a blob, and that blob just kept blobbing and splitting and evolving and getting swept around by waves in the oceans.

Maybe some other blobs developed at the same time thousands of miles away in another part of the world. Maybe some goo was introduced by that asteroid that shook things up a bit. Whatever the case, a LOT of blobby activity was going on, and those blobs all had to survive, so that one magical day many of the blobs washed up on a shore and started to sproing into monkeys like some sort of Darwinian Jiffy-Pop.

Anyway, I sort of digress, but you get the picture. Everyone, and I do mean *everyone*, has – in an EXTREMELY long list that predates everything – an ass-load of family that has already "been there done that." They have dodged saber-tooths, microbes, natural disasters, other peoples, and maybe even some dinosaurs (Great GREAT Uncle Xaaagch could spin a yarn – that Ol' Gray-Berry-Eater – so we ain't so sure about the whole "dinosaur" story).

But our families have survived, they jumped across that giant crack when the continents split apart, walked – uphill and through the snow – over that land bridge, took a sharp right at the ice age, maybe two or three of them were ridiculed and cast out because they believed in their hearts that eating the brains of the conquered gave them the powers of said conquered.

I mean... they been through The Shit.

And they kept having babies, and the babies lived, and thrived, and everyone kept plodding to the Right.

And that ploddination, by and by, came down to You. Me.

I do not have to hunt giant birds or mastodons for food; I have to find an inexpensive steak at the HEB for dinner. I no longer have to (I don't *have* to) tear the heart out of a neighbor and thwop it on a flat stone and smear the blood on my face to avoid The Boils; I just wear a mask and wash my hands 26 times a day.

And I wonder, in awe, how and where certain traits found their way down to me – you know, the ones that make people ask if perhaps I have brain damage or something. Like the time I got new sneakers for the start of the school year, I was maybe 7. I noticed how they made me able to run faster and jump higher and farther than ever before.

To prove it, I went running out of the house on Mohawk Lake, down the gravel driveway, hit the very edge of the two-lane road and LAUNCHED myself into the air, landing just on the other side of the double yellow line that separated the lanes.

"BOOM!" I thought to myself, "I am The Bionic Man with these new sho..."

My brag fest was cut short by a *really* loud screech of car brakes, which immediately made me whip my head to the right, where a Volvo had stopped maybe 16 inches from me; I actually reached out and touched the hood. The driver's eyes were now about seven inches wider than they were designed to be.

I honestly can't remember if I was more scared or impressed by the fact that I just stopped a Volvo with one hand. But in either case, I took off running down toward the lake, and then onto the railroad tracks, super satisfied with my new sneakers.

Or perhaps one day I wanted to see how a bullet worked, and if it could *only* be activated by a gun. I grabbed a .22 shell, went out onto the back porch, set the shell on the concrete floor facing the concrete lip where it met the rest of the house. I cracked a hammer down on the base of the shell, and hell YEAH.

The bullet *pinged* off the lip on the concrete floor and *zinged* back past my ear before I even became aware that my high-probability-of-self-elimination-scientific-theory had just been proven.

I have had a few close calls like that in my life, and each time I have one, I think of the others. I think of my ancestors, lined up like reflections in a mirror facing another mirror that goes on forever, each ancestor slapping their forehead going "Jesus Christ, THIS is what we worked so hard to get to?" All the way back to Great Grandpa Glonk and Great Grandma Chargk, as they double-take a look at each other and say at the same time,

"He gets that from YOUR side..."

LUCKY ME

In high school, I had never been convicted of shying away from some mild pot-stirring or good-natured dickery on occasion. And I most certainly used humor as a protective Rubber-Chicken Dome against the onslaught of the social ICBMs that life launched at me in general.

But I was not in any way a big instigator. By that, I mean I did not go around like some kind of double-Y'ed Diogenes searching for a fight all the time. As a matter of fact, I have never liked conflict. If there was a path marked "avoidance, this way," I took it at a sprint.

As luck would have it, though, I still seemed to have the face, the attitude, or the aura that just invited stupid shit upon me. Usually in the form of some sort of threatening behavior that I did not precipitate.

Sometimes it was as innocuous as thinking someone was joking around – but they weren't – so I joked back, and then the first person wanted to kick my ass.

That very specific thing has happened to me more than a few times. One time that sticks in my head the most, for some reason, was in the locker room in high school. Me and three other friends were hanging out before practice, trash-talking our wrestling coach and school in general. We were just leaning on the end of a row of lockers for at least 30 minutes, during which time some other athletes had come in, changed, and headed to their field or gym space.

And there we still were, same position, just yapping and laughing.

Until this one guy started banging his fist on his locker – it appeared like someone had broken in and stolen some of his shit. The reason we guessed this was because he slammed his locker door and yelled,

"Who the fuck broke into my locker and stole some of my shit?!"

The four of us looked over toward him, standing there seething in just his uniform pants and his mesh crop top, all six foot two of him, red-faced sinew straining on his neck, biceps flexing like he was ready to kill somebody.

"What happened, Shawn (not his real name)," one of my friends asked, genuinely concerned.

Shawn glared over at us

"Did you not just hear me? Someone broke into my locker and stole my shit. My brand-new cleats, my shoulder pads... a whole bunch of shit."

We four did not know what to say, we had been standing there gossiping for awhile, and we did not see anyone do anything that looked like breaking in or shit-stealing. We told Shawn so.

This did not seem to help matters. Shawn strode over to us with murder in his eyes.

"If I catch who did this, I'm going to kick his ass, and he's going to wish he was dead."

And then he glared *right... at... me*.

He stared for enough seconds that it was clear he thought *I had done it*. I raised an eyebrow, glanced at my friends, who stood there wondering what the hell.

"Sure hope you don't find out it was me then, heh heh heh" I offered, thinking... You know, I have no idea why I thought *that* particular remark would have been helpful at *that* moment in time.

Shawn just kept glaring at me, one curled lip away from a regulation snarling.

Now, I had a reputation around school, and I owned that. I had a mouth, and I had a sense of humor that was, admittedly, not for everyone. But I had never had a rep of being a thief or that particular flavor of delinquent.

Shawn just would not let it go, he obviously had a hard-on for me being the perpetrator.

"Yeah?" he grimaced through his teeth liked Clint Eastwood, "Alright then."

And then he puffed out his chest and stormed out of the locker room.

My friends and I just stood there for a few seconds, eyes darting back and forth to each other, actually not knowing what to say. Then we went right back to just doing what we had been doing.

A few minutes later, Shawn stormed back in, walked right up to me, almost touching noses (he had to bend a bit to reach my nose with his), and growled,

"Where the fuck were you, man?"

I had no working idea what he was talking about.

"Wait a minute... wh... what...?" I said.

He shifted on his feet and got as close as he could before he would have been on the other side of me

"You said you stole my shit, I said let's go outside and take care of this. I waited, and I came back in here and you're still standing here."

Okay, so I *did* know how to keep my mouth shut and not provoke giant, angry people to some extent, but there was just so much I *really* wanted to say in answer to that fine representation of the actions that had occurred in the past eleven minutes as Shawn saw them. Fortunately for me, one of my friends spoke up before my mouth could engage without the loving care of my brain.

"Shawn, what the hell, man. He never said..."

"Are you calling me a liar?" Shawn shot back.

"Man, I didn't take your shit." I said.

"Then why did you say you did..."

This ridiculous conversation went back and forth for a bit before a sad realization came upon me. In that situation, Shawn was way angrier than he was smart, and he REALLY wanted to hit somebody.

I wound up having to apologize to him for making a humorous quip, and not treating the situation with the seriousness it demanded. Between the four of us, we were able to convince Shawn that we had been standing there for a long while, and did not see anyone near his locker, but if we heard anything, we would let him know.

As he stomped away to the coach's office, we decided it was a good time to not be there anymore.

But it never left me... why was I the one that Shawn focused on there? There were four of us, we were all on some team... football, wrestling, soccer... what made that big angry guy zoom in on me, activating my natural defense-response, which happened to be a SkyNet of snark and humor?

I can't even say that it's just the way I looked all the time, because it happened even when there was no in-person activity. Just weird-assed situations that would pop up out of nowhere and soon have me gawking at the business end of tree-trunk arms and wrecking-ball fists. Just flat-out dumb-luck shit.

I had a friend at Busch Gardens named Bob. Bob and I used to hang out with Allan a lot after work. We were all pretty much nerds, and we all were in denial. We also all had a bit of a crush on this pretty young woman named Heidi. Allan and I knew Heidi because she worked in our section of the park, and Bob knew her by extension because we knew her.

One Friday night, the four of us were going to a party hosted by another person who worked at Busch. We met up in the parking lot, Bob was going to take Heidi in his car (well-played, Bob), I was riding shotgun with Allan, and we were to follow them.

Bob and Heidi were in his powder blue VW Bug. Easy to follow in the days before cell phones and GPS. Bob and Heidi pulled out of the lot in their powder blue VW Bug, and Allan and I pulled out right behind them.

We stopped at a light, where we made faces at each other back and forth between the cars, then continued to follow them, making one big left hand turn in a busy intersection as we went, always keeping our eyes on that powder blue VW Bug.

Wellllll, after about twenty minutes of heading down increasingly smaller roads and weird turns, Allan and I started asking each other out loud what *exactly* the hell it was Bob was doing, and where he was taking us. When we got to some *very* rural country, we both were getting a bit pissed, but also a tad frightened.

"Wait a minute," Allan said, "He's gotta be lost. What the hell?"

Then Bob's powder blue VW Bug pulled into a little gravel offshoot from what was, by then, *laughably* referred to as the "Main Road." His car came to a stop, the driver side door opened, and out stepped the biggest human being we had ever seen.

This kid was easily six foot six, and looked like he could beat up an entire grade level with one punch. His letter jacket had stripes and medals all over it from three or four different sports; his flattop haircut was so stiff you could card wool on it.

He lumbered over to Allan's small, reliable, sensible car – it seemed like we were at eye-level with his kneecaps. He leaned down and stared in at us like we were his next meal. I am positive to this day that the abject fear he saw in our eyes made him dial down his murderosity to about 30%.

"What's up guys? There a reason you been following me the past twenty minutes?" he said, surprisingly good-natured for such a perfect killing machine.

Allan and I just looked at each other, both rather dumbstruck with our mouths agape; Allan made a vague gesture toward the behemoth's vehicle, neither one of us could form a sentence.

"We... were following... a friend... to a party," Allan stammered.

"Dude, you are literally in the same car he was driving... we never took our eyes off you, I mean them," I explained, trying desperately to make sense of this beautifully staged cross between a David Copperfield Illusion and a teen slasher flick like WRONG TURN.

The Mountain smiled a bit, nodded his head. I guess that made sense to him. Plus he could probably smell the urine puddling in our vinyl bucket seats.

"Okay, no harm. You know how to get back out to the highway?" he sincerely asked.

Then he started to walk back to his VW. *Then he stopped*. We saw his body language change; he stood up straight, his head tilted back slightly as he took a deep breath. Then he turned around and started to walk back toward us. We just sat there and watched, too dumb to even hit reverse and peel out of that death trap.

This is it, I thought. This is where Body Count movies get their ideas from: this scary, ripped-from-the-headlines story that will act like a cautionary tale for teens for decades to come. I envisioned his hand plunging down through the top of the car, grabbing both our heads in one gargantuan palm, a hard twist, and *off they came*.

Instead of ripping our heads from the rest of our bodies, Monolith laughed as he leaned over once again.

"Ah," he said, "I think I know exactly where you got lost."

He proceeded to tell us about that big left hand turn we made at the busy intersection, and said he only remembered it because of the ridiculous circumstances.

The intersection was where five roads all converged, and he had gotten blocked by another car, so he sped around it, traveling from (our) right to left. The road we were on, following *actual* Bob and Heidi, was on a bit of a curve to the right as we approached the same intersection, so we didn't see Bob turn *right* at the light as we rounded the corner – we just saw The Hulk going *left* through the light. He said he remembers this, because he saw the same *exact* car he was driving turn into the direction he was coming *from*.

And I shit you not, when he finished he looked at us and laughed,

"You guys had me scared there for a minute!"

He shook our hands, and we parted.

Allan's hands were still shaking when we pulled onto the highway. We were absolutely flabbergasted as to how and why THAT had just happened.

We gave it the correct amount of thought, then came to the conclusion that we had nothing left to do but shrug it off and go get a beer. We missed the party, but worst of all, we were severely pissed that Bob wound up hanging out with Heidi all night. *Presumably.*

Sometimes you just can't catch a break, but a break gets shoved upon you anyway. I mean, do you have any idea how many stars had to align for that to happen? The probabilities that had to be wined and dined, the physics of relative ground speeds on straight and curved lines, circumferences and drag coefficients of tires... just so that Allan and I could be scared shitless and confused beyond words? Are you *kidding* me?

The hind-sight of it all, though, which I did realize eventually, was that the *real* luck was NOT having every bone in our bodies snapped like dry kindling, and being stuffed into a shallow, leaf-covered grave out in the woods in Colonial Williamsburg. So overall, I was good with them odds.

KNOWING IS THE FIRST STEP

We've all played The Game. It may have been early in life, or later in life, and we may have all come to different conclusions, but we've all played "What Would I Do in That Situation."

We have watched games on TV or in person, or shows or movies, and shouted stupid Arm-Chair Quarterback/ Actor remarks at those who are actually playing. Useful remarks like,

"Are you kidding me?! Not up the middle, put it in the air,"

or

"*Really*, you don't know the answer to *that* question,"

or

"Do NOT open that DOOR!"

or even

"I would *never* have done *that*... not in a MILLION years."

But the truth – the sad truth – is that we would never know what we would do until we were in the same (or similar) situation in real life.

Now I have known a few folks in my life that seemed like they were just *born* knowing who they were and what was up at a really young age. They just seem to *get it*, and they respond in what appears to be a reasonable and virtuous manner, and it doesn't even matter the odds or what's at stake. They just *know* how to behave.

Conversely, there are a group of humans who just NEVER seem to get it. They always react in the wrong way, the shitty way, the least helpful way, the stupid way, and they never give it a second thought – give themselves a second thought.

And then there is the Average Bear cross-section of humanity, who could go either way: it takes them longer to even figure *that* out. That's most of us, and that's where I fall. I have never claimed to be the smartest crayon in the tool shed, and when I was younger I almost never – in my own opinion, from years of data – got it right.

I would see things that I *knew* to be wrong, at least with my limited understanding of the people and the world, and my own set of morals, mores and beliefs, and I would hesitate too long, or upon a request to help out the infracted party... did not. It's always very difficult to talk or even think about these days, but I was a huge dumbass wuss when it came to that sort of thing.

Even at my age now, I still see plenty of times when I don't think I did enough, or reacted rather poorly when seeing some sort of injustice perpetrated. Though I feel like I have gotten to a place where I notice it in the moment and try to mitigate more. It just doesn't come naturally, and it bothers me a LOT.

But I have had a lot more practice and experience over the years to inform my actions now, which makes it that much more terrifying to think back on those times that helped form me.

A couple instances in my yute make me cringe the most. There are times when I think I'm totally Hot Shit, that I *purposefully* call those moments back to mind, just to keep me grounded. I also feel, no matter how wonderfully anyone thinks they handled something, there is always room for improvement, as well as room to try to look at things from a different angle of view, to try to get better clarity.

When I was in middle school, I had this friend; we were not close, tight, ride-or-die friends, but we used to hang out. I thought he was an alright guy. He was an Irish kid, like IRISH Irish – the accent, the look – named Steve. His family had just moved to Saranac Lake from Chicago, I think. He was a bit of a rough-around-the-edges kind of guy, wasn't too afraid of anything or anyone, always stood up for himself – the opposite of me at the time. This tended to immediately attract the attention – not in a good way – of the regular bullies at the school.

One day, some friends and I were doing the downtown thing during lunch, and we were on our way back to the school, walking up the rocky slope from the river to the top of the hill where the overpass would take us right back to school property. We noticed a small group of four kids halfway up the hill. One of them was Steve, the others were the Punks, all older than me, and a lot bigger.

Harsh words were being passed back and forth, mostly from one of the bigger kids who I knew vaguely; his two toadies shouted a lot of "yeahs" and "uh-HUHs" and other meaningful nuggets. As we got closer, the two main performers (Steve and Mr. Big) decided to "settle this like men" and took off their coats and squared up. Steve made REALLY short work of Mr. Big – laid him out on the ground like a pro boxer.

"JEEZUM CROW." Was the only thing I thought. "Wow," may have been in there somewhere, as well. By the time my group was passing them, Steve was already putting on his coat, and getting ready to head back to school. We nodded at each other as I passed. Mind you, I had never really participated in an honest, fair, two-way fist fight. I had no clue what the rules were, or how to behave after one took place. But I know for a fact that what happened next was definitely *not* following the rules of gentlemanly sportsmanship.

From behind us I heard one of the toadies shout,

"NOBODY beats up MY friend!" in a very indignant manner, followed by some more fisticuff sounds.

By the time my group had turned back around, the other two toadies were all over Steve's shit with extreme vengeance. He got his ass handed to him, even though he defended himself better than I had ever seen anyone close to my age do before. It was his turn to be on the ground, now also getting kicked – and then Mr. Big jumped up and *stomped* on Steve's back, kicked him once more, then spat on him. And then the three took off up the hill past us to return to school, making sure to slow down briefly to glare at my group and growl the requisite,

"What are YOU looking at, pussies?"

And I just stood there.

We all just stood there.

Not a finger was raised.

After what felt like hours, two of us, myself included, walked back down to Steve to help him up, the others in our group just ran back up the hill to school. Steve was pretty trashed. Bloody nose, scrapes and red marks that turned to bruises later, and both eyes swollen shut, snot mixing with blood from his nose, the whole nine yards.

He regained his footing, brushed himself off a tiny bit, then shrugged his arms out of our hands, never looked us in the eye, and he coarsely coughed out,

"Go to hell!" then stumbled up the hill at a quicker pace than I would have expected from his condition.

My friend and I just side-eyed each other, perhaps feeling guilty that we really did nothing to help him, despite the odds, perhaps each hoping the other would have something to say that was pertinent to the situation. We did not.

Not too much later that day, during a class, I got called to the Office. This time it was not for something I, personally, had done, though. When I got into Principal Blumetti's office, guess who else was there. Yeah. Steve and the Three Pricks. Here was the chance to redeem myself, and help get some sort of justice done.

I had no idea what happened, did Steve finger those three guys and have them called into the office? Did one of my other friends from the hill report the incident? I didn't see any of them, so I was clueless.

Blumetti made a short, fairly angry introduction of the situation I already knew had happened, then he looked me in the eye and asked me to corroborate the fact that these three dickheads did what was reported to have happened.

And again... Deer-in-Headlights was all I had to offer.

This had nothing to do with "not being a narc, or snitch, or even a stool pigeon," this was again just fear and dumbshittery on my part. I am absolutely certain I actually stammered some bullshit, but never formed a complete sentence.

The fact that the Three Pricks stared my ass down with nothing but death in their eyes had very little to do with it. I just plain had no idea what was the right thing to do.

The Principal rolled his eyes, genuinely furious that he could not get any proof of what happened, even knowing the reputation these punks had. I could get zero reading off of Steve, who never looked at me once.

Blumetti waved his hand in my general direction,

"Get out of here," he spat.

I hesitated a moment, then my legs found some strength to move me out, and I went back to class. Even as I sat back in my chair in Science class, I had no idea what I had just done... or failed to do. I was completely at a loss.

Steve never came back to school, and to this day I have no idea what ever happened with him – clearly he transferred to another school. All that ever ran through my mind for literal YEARS after that incident, and my behavior therein, was three words:

"What a Puss."

The other three turds never really bothered me much afterward; I guess they figured I did them a huge favor one way or the other, Code of Silence-wise. I suppose I had earned a Bully Pass.

But it was shit like that that helped me understand that sometimes you had to fight back, whether for yourself or for someone else who was being unfairly and overwhelmingly attacked. It took awhile, but it sank in.

When I was much older, married and had kids, in my thirties, I was working on Sixth Street in Austin as an improv performer at a famous venue. We had five shows a week: Thursday, Friday and Saturday. Saturday's shows were during The Zoo, which was what we called Sixth Street after 9pm on the weekends. That stretch of Sixth was closed to car traffic from Congress avenue down to I-35, and it was NUTS.

By the time our second show ended at around 10:30 or 11pm, the street was an undulating python of humanity – not all bent on crime, but certainly full of life and alcohol and other recreational substances and thoughts.

Between our two shows and after our last were Open Mic sets, where a lot of comics we knew took the stage and generally hung out drinking and talking and whatnot. On this night, one of our improv group had to head home right after the last show. I was walking her to her car parked around the corner on Red River Street, and we passed the mouth of the back alley to the theater.

As we walked past, we heard some noise from the big green industrial dumpster in the weeds, the joyless sounds of partying coming back up-and-out, hitting the ground with a wet splatter. Then this young woman in a flower-print dress staggered to her feet and started to head down the alley toward the light of the cross-street Neches at the far end.

"Just another night of too much fun," we may have both thought to ourselves at first blush, but we didn't even have time to finish the thought, or even head over to make sure she was okay.

Five young men who were walking a distance behind us, having just turned off Sixth Street, were heading to the parking area and spotted her. It was absolutely blood-chilling how the five of them, *as a whole*, immediately zeroed in on her, and turned down the alley after her like some sort of murmuration of shitheads. They clearly did not have plans on helping her, judging from the cat-calls and bullshit they shouted as they gained on her.

"CRAP," said my friend.

"CRAP," I echoed. "Go see if you can find a cop."

"SHIIIIIIIT shit shit shit," she hissed as she headed back out toward Sixth Street to flag down one or more of the bike cops that patrolled the area all the time... though never when you actually needed one.

"And hurry," I yelled to her as I headed over to the alley, as if I had to even say it. I was not anxious to be in that alley with those assholes... but I bet I was not going to have it as rough as the woman they were following. As the five guys closed in on her, she had fallen down half-way across the alley; it looked like I had very few options.

"Well... FUCK." I snarled to myself, and headed in toward them.

The guys had already circled the unfortunate woman, who was trying to stand up, and were spewing the lines of stupid, abusive thugs who thought they were going to have some fun at someone else's expense.

"Hey baby, you lost?"

"You want a good time, honey?"

And like-minded boilerplate sociopathic garbage.

I was within ten or fifteen feet of them, scanning the alley for something I could use, a chunk of wood, a pipe, anything. And then one of them saw me coming, and made sure the rest of his cronies did too.

Then they turned toward me. And I stopped dead in my tracks.

They started a slow menacing surge toward me; their leader, for lack of a better word, started asking me if I had a death wish, or if I was stupid, and another suggested a smart person would turn around and walk away.

I just stood there, as they shuffled closer, and the Leader's hand went to his waistband

"Bitch, I got something for you, if you dumb enough to want it," he said as his strutting shape got closer. His buddies started to fan out to the sides, and I figured this was it for me... but I wasn't moving.

Then something weird happened. All of them, all at once, got a looser look about them. Their shoulders dropped, and as they came into what little light was thrown into alley from the back door lights of the theater and the lone street light at the corner on Red River. I could see most of them avert their gaze from me, and start to saunter in a path that led *past* me, not *into* me.

Me? CLUELESS. I knew I certainly was not the sort of figure that frightened five guys with a gun away from an Ass-Kicking Party with no cover charge.

As the crew headed past me back out onto Red River, the Leader never gave up the bravado, patting his waistband and letting me know how it was going to end for me if I didn't move.

"Last chance Motherfucker, you think I'm afraid of

you?" he spat.

And then he reached me, didn't even pause, he just shouldered roughly past me, still patting his waistband, and strutted out to join his buddies. I turned slightly to my left to watch them all turn the corner onto Red River and head toward Fifth Street, then I shot a glance back toward the woman, who had now made it to the opposite end of the alley and back out into the light on Neches.

I sighed a HUGE sigh of relief, doubled-over, with my hands on my knees; and then I stood up and turned around to my right.

There on the back stoop of the theater stood six or seven of my improv friends and some stand-up comics in the pool of light. Some of these guys I didn't even particularly get along with real well. I will not lie, part of me has always thought that the truth of the situation was none of them could turn down the opportunity to see me get beaten to a pulp. But there they were. Never had I been so glad to see comedians in my entire life.

"You alright," said Howard, one of the comics who always seemed a little tough to me. "If he had a gun you'd be dead by now. He's all talk," and then he headed back into the theater.

Around the corner came the friend I had been walking to her car.

"Holy shit!" she sighed, "I couldn't find a cop in time, so I told these guys what was happening."

"You guys could have let me know you were there," I

choked. "I think I actually shit my pants."

Then we had a good laugh, though mine was all nerves. Two bike cops rolled up a few seconds later, asked what was going on, and one headed down the other end of the alley to see what up. The other asked for specifics, and once again I had none to give, other than the print of the woman's dress. It was dark, I saw nothing else – the whole time my eye was on the Leader's waist band, and his buddies knew enough to look away when they came into the light. The cop gave me a look, a look I had seen before. He was not buying it.

"Why don't you save your bullshit," I said in my head. "You guys are never around when you're needed."

But I wasn't really too pissed off. I mean there were only *so many* bike cops, and there were vastly more humans sloshing around on Sixth Street than they could *possibly* keep up with. The chances of them being close by when this happened were slim at best. I was just upset because of the discomfort it caused me. The woman was more than likely safer out in the Zoo now with more people around. She was okay, and I was okay.

Most importantly, though... was that now I knew.

OH GIPPER, WHERE ART THOU?

Athleticism, much like The Force, was never strong with me. I was in pretty decent shape in high school, don't get me wrong – a bunch of years doing the type of work one does on a farm had its perks. But I didn't have the *mindset* for sports, and spent most of my time pre-high school alone doing chores or playing. I had little to no idea of how to work toward a common goal with a bunch of kids wearing uniforms.

Team sports, where you had to play whatever game it was with others, helping each other out to make the goal, score the point, achieve the win... were a foreign concept to me. You know, passing the ball, blocking the opponents, running the leg of a relay or what have you.

If you ask me, I think some sports just go *way* too far in giving stats about team involvement anyway. Take hockey, where *this* player scores a goal, but *that* player assisted with the goal, and *these* players were also on the ice during the assists that would forthwith become the goal being scored. I mean really, technically, shouldn't *every* team member be credited with an assist, weren't they all out there *literally* assisting when the one-who-scored scored?

All I know is it felt like too much pressure to have to rely on, or be relied upon to help someone else do the thing they had to do on the field or in the gym. What if I screwed up? What if I was the reason the other team got the ball and scored against us? What if I just plain did not understand the cues my team member was trying to give me, and I ZIGGED when, Jesus H Christ, T-Bone was clearly telegraphing a ZAG? Wasn't he?

T-Bone could be a bit of a loose cannon.

I played Little League Baseball for less than half of one summer, when I was back in Mohawk Lake. Our team was this little rag-tag ensemble that you might imagine when thoughts came to rest on small town sports.

Our practice (and game day) field was the overgrown area of the playground at the Mohawk Lake Elementary School, out there in the tree line, directly across from the Mohawk Lake Cemetery. In fact, if any of us were power hitters, it would have been possible to drive one down the third base line right into the gravestone of some player's family member.

If the catcher missed a ball, it went directly into the

woods. In fact, I got my start running down errant forest balls when my older brothers were playing. Wild pitch, catcher got a piece of it – just enough to deflect it over his head and into the pines.

"Hey, you," the catcher would say while pointing his glove in my direction, "go grab that, huh?"

I would snap out of my scintillating discussion with a butterfly in the sun-bleached, barely standing, original General Doubleday-built dugout, and look over to the home plate for clarification,

"Who... Me?"

"Yeah, you... jeezum crow, go find that, we only have three."

And thus my baseball career started, and I proved so good at finding the ol' horsehide that went careening into the old growth forest, the coach asked me to come by on whatever day it was that the little kids played. I said, meh, okay.

I quickly learned that Right Field was my jam, because who the hell ever hit to Right Field? But this is where I also found out that team sports were not for me.

First Base was this kid named Dicky, and Dicky had what used to be called a Lazy Eye. Like *wicked* lazy. Any time I had to throw to him, or when we were just practicing and he had to throw to me, I could never tell *where* he was looking, or why.

So I would constantly try to adjust where *I was* in relation to *his gaze*, and not only did this aggravate

Dicky, but Coach Strack must have thought I had a learning disability.

And so ended my baseball career.

Basketball? Too short and no clue what any of it meant.

Football? Too small to be much of a lineman, not fast or coordinated enough to be a receiver. Took me all of preseason practice one year in high school to figure that out.

Hockey?

Couldn't skate well enough and wasn't aggressive enough.

Lacrosse?

Same as Hockey, but no skates and on grass.

Cross-Country, Track and Field, Skiing, Soccer?

Nope nope nopitty nope.

Wrestling? *Hmm*.

When I finally got into it at the end of my tenth grade year, it seemed to be a pretty good fit. I would be on a team, but I would just be competing one-on-one. And also by the time I tried out for wrestling, I was much bigger and stronger than I was in my Little League days. The only thing I never seemed to really click with was the mental game.

I was good enough when it came down to strength, and was pretty good even when it came down to finesse. But when it came to a straight-up even match of strength and skill, I never seemed to have that extra *whatever the hell it was* that made winners.

But it really didn't matter, because I wasn't in it for the big wins. Oh sure, I loved it when I pinned an opponent in under 20 seconds; the crowd going wild was always a boost. But I never really had any dreams for some sort of Gipper-esque career-defining All-American prowess kind of career. I found it was the fun of being on the team: practicing, complaining, hanging out with a bunch of other unruly guys on away games and tournaments that was my fuel. It did not take long to get me asking, "where has this camaraderie been all my life?"

Between the testosterone-driven practices and workouts, the occasional (light) trashing of a Motel 6 room involving a few cans of Chef Boy-Ar-Dee Beef Ravioli, the sneaking out of the hotel at night to try to find the hotel where the cheerleaders were staying, and the once-in-a-while rush of an almost mall fight, there were some great times had in the name of Teamwork.

"Making Weight" was the big thing in wrestling. Everyone on the team wrestled at a certain weight class, and you could be under that weight, but not over... not even by a single ounce.

If you had a spot on the team very close to what your walking around weight was, that was groovy, very little effort there. Walking around at 140 but wrestling at 138 or even 132, pretty easy. You could even wrestle up a class or two if you cared to, say walk around at 140 pounds, but wrestle at 155 or 167.

But I cruised at 155, and in order to have a spot on the

Varsity team I had to slim down to 132. A lot of weight loss, at the early stages, is just water weight that we all have, that first ten or fifteen pounds can go pretty quick. But that last eight? That takes some doing.

And the last 8 *ounces*? That can damn-near be parts of your body and soul coming off. I have known wrestlers who had to run into the locker room to shave themselves completely smooth to make weight for tournaments.

The season was in the fall/winter, so Thanksgiving and Christmas always happened, and if you had to lose a lot of weight for the tournaments that coincided with these holidays – like I did – it was murder to sit around watching others eat. My holiday meals were a LOT of grapefruit and rice cakes.

It became an obsession, but it also was a little fun and sometimes a tad weird and dangerous, but almost always a challenge met with grit, determination, and creativity.

And we absolutely always had the support of the team to keep us going.

For the normal times, I had my friend Jeff who got me into the sport. We'd regularly walk or run a lot around Bethel Manor, as we both lived there. If we needed to lose weight a bit faster, we'd put on our plastic suits and run-walk-run-walk for an hour or so. Plastic suits were a staple – a lightweight, heavy gauge plastic sweatshirt and pants that held in heat and made you sweat like crazy.

When you were really up against it, you could hop in the heated whirlpool for a few minutes to get your body temp up, then don the plastics and go run. If you were feeling particularly insane, the plastics could be worn in a sauna. For an extra Russian Roulette feel, Ex-Lax could be added to any of these above activities.

We had a tournament up in Richmond one season, about an hour and a half or so away. I was still about a quarter pound over weight, and my first match was in a few hours. Someone else had some weight to shed as well, so on the drive up, Coach made us put on the plastics and get out of the van. He drove very slow with his hazard lights on, and we ran behind the van on the side of the road for 15 minute intervals.

Gary and Todd, a couple State-Level winners, opened the doors at the back of the van and Gary slapped one of his Rolling Stones cassettes into a boombox and they held it facing us to keep us entertained, yelling encouragement and jokes at us the whole time. I swear we ran almost a third of the distance to Richmond.

When we got to the host school, Coach – in front of everybody – and after I weighed in (just barely underweight) told me he was benching me, and hoped I had learned a valuable lesson. Indeed I had, and that lesson was: *Coach was an asshole.*

This sort of thing would happen often enough that we learned to get a little mad... and then get a little even.

Now I am certain that there were plenty of ol' Knute Rocknes out there, coaches that inspired and were well-loved and respected, but our coach was not really one of them. Don't get me wrong, he had his moments, but overall, he was rather taken with himself and was far more concerned with showing us how awesome he was than making us better athletes and people. And he could be a petty, sadistic little prick, too.

When one's mind needed to be taken off the whole bullshit actions of our Coach, there were extracurricular activities that could be woven into the weight loss regimen.

My friends Tom and Rob, another guy named Russ (who was insane), and I would, on occasion – especially when Coach had a bug up his ass and had been particularly bitchy in practice and threatened us with being removed from our chosen weight class because we weren't "being serious about making weight," – have a snack of ex-lax, put on our sweats with plastics over the top, and drive around while waiting for that special moment when weight would be expelled unceremoniously and with great verve.

On such a night, we purchased cartons of eggs at the Big Star in Heritage Square, and drove to the coach's house. We made a U-turn in the cul-de-sac at the end of his street, pulled up next to his house, got out, shouted a thing or two about what he should suck, how long and how hard. Then we threw as many eggs as we could in ten seconds, jumped back in the car and sped off before the first egg even hit a window.

The main problem with this plan – other than the complete lack of strategization – was that the only entrance/exit to coach's street was at a T in the road. And, in the state of rapid egress that we occupied after the minimal low-level law-breaky mischief, Rob failed to recall that it was indeed a T.

The Gremlin jumped the ditch on the other side of the narrow two-lane road, landed with a crunch in some scraggly grass and dirt, causing a cloud of dust to impair the driver's vision just enough so that when he finally slammed on the brakes and allowed said dust to clear, everyone in the vehicle noticed that the tires of the car were now straddling a grave, and the headlights made it possible to read the marker quite well.

Needless to say, slamming the car into reverse, doing a donut or two before finding the road again in the new dust cloud, and then peeling out of the graveyard in immediate and desperate need of finding a bathroom, was not anyone's finest hour.

But I'm sure, each of us – in our own way – felt like we were up against it that night; felt like the breaks were beating us, and yet still... we went out there with all we had... and won just one... for the Gipper.

And we were happy.

THE
CIRCLE
OF
(MILLER
HIGH)
LIFE

When I was in college – this is at UNLV in Las Vegas – I drank a bit. Now you may say to yourself, "well, duh... we ALL drank a bit in college. So what?" I get the feeling it may have been a bit *more* than a *bit* with me. Might even have been what some folks call "a lot," or an alternate spelling of "A LOT." Perhaps even "A LOT A LOT."

The degree to which I drank, and this is mostly beer we're talking about here, was especially notable because of where and when I started and how quickly I got up to almost a case of beer a night at the age of 18.

I very vividly recall the first time I "got drunk." It was in high school, as with a lot of folks, and it was something of a surprise to me that I did so when and where I did. See, up until tenth grade, I never drank, nor even entertained imbibing, tippling, guzzling, sipping, or even quaffing *any* alcohol. Sure, I had seen my share of drinking – my dad drank, my grandfather drank, a few of my friends at school drank (or claimed they did anyway). But I never did, not once; it held no allure for me.

In the summer between tenth and eleventh grade, a group of us kids were "hanging out," in the traditional sense. We all lived in the base housing area up the road from Langley Air Force Base in Virginia. It was me, a few of my nerd friends, the daughter of a base chaplain whom one of my friends was dating, and her brother, the local stoner and "I know a Guy" Guy.

We were milling about the parking lot of the multi-denominational church, which was, by the way, a few short yards from the house of the base chaplain. We were playing grab-ass and talking shit, trying to figure out what to do with the rest of the evening, when the chaplain's daughter's brother – The Guy – excused himself for a moment, and subsequently returned with a bottle of the good stuff.

Thunderbird by name, marketed to a generation of consumers who appreciate easy drinkability at a fair price by design. This "wine," for lack of a better, more accurate term, was clearly something a high school student could easily get a hold of. We weren't sniffing any corks. Or caps.

The bottle, she was opened, the Genie was released, it got passed around, and in turn came to me.

"No. No, thank you," I said, passing it to Mike on my right. "I don't drink."

This response drew some odd looks from my friends, not because I didn't drink, but because they all thought, what with the way I was, surely I *must* have been a drinker. But no, I assured them, don't touch the stuff.

I got some pretty typical support from these fine kids as the bottle began its second revolution around the circle:

"Seriously? Dorchak doesn't drink?" Glug.

"What are you, some sort of prude?" Glug glug.

"Are you Amish?" Gluggity glug.

"Fag." Double glug.

Now I have never really been one to start or stop doing something just because of peer pressure, mostly because I was not aware of what that term was at 15; however, I now had a sudden urge to see what all the fuss was about. And also, I didn't want my peers to think I was some sort of prudish Amish fag who didn't drink.

I took the bottle, almost 2/3 empty now of its dark, mystery-flavored liquid, and took a decent size pull from it. Mmmmmmmm.

Surprisingly, I did not die. And B) I was not enamored of the taste, nor aftertaste. But I was, after a few more sips, interested in this new activity I was just initiated into. And I wanted to explore it a bit more.

Fortunately, I knew a Guy.

In the pursuit of the social sciences, my buddy Jeff and I decided we wanted to get drunk – safely, and privately – to see what all the fuss was about. You never go full drunkard for the first time at a party with a bunch of strangers or coworkers. So our Guy hooks us up.

"Alright, man!" he grinned – in a way that only someone who has smoked a LOT of weed by the time they were 14 years old can smile – and he started to show us the plan as he dragged one finger on the palm of his other hand,

"Okay, man, here's the deal. You know that chain link fence behind my house, over near the spillway? Well, you put twenty bucks in a brown paper lunch bag, and you shove it through the hole at the bottom of the fence. Come see me on Friday during lunch, I'll tell you the rest."

Simple, straightforward plan, that in no way could go wrong or end in danger or jail time. We agreed. We stuffed the twenty bucks in bag, and stuffed the bag through hole in fence under the bushes.

On Friday, at lunch, we find The Guy hanging out in the Stoner Lounge, off the lunch room/commons area. He tells us ,

"Two o'clock, man. Have fun!"

Jeff and I look at each other, then back to The Guy for some more explanation.

"Two o'clock," he repeats, as if we understood

more from the same thing being said a second time, still without any extra words of clarification.

He then went on to explain to us that "orders" would be filled and placed in a semi-circle under that bush behind the fence. The order of placement was like a clock dial from Nine to Three. You reach in at "two o'clock," whatever you felt there was yours. You did not know what you were getting, just whatever Rock could get for 5 bucks, while he pocketed the rest for his trouble. Rock would make sure you got something good.

Rock was that kid that everyone knew one of; you know that guy of indeterminate age, who could easily pass for 17, 21, 35, or maybe even a 40 year old 21 Jump Street Undercover Narc type of guy. He had an easy time buying alcohol at the 7-11 just down the road from the Church. Nobody questioned him, this over six foot, dark-skinned, rather handsome bald guy, who sauntered everywhere like he owned the place and knew everybody. He was actually a pretty nice guy; dated my sister for a bit, we got along fine.

On the big day, which I believe was Saturday night for Jeff and me, we went to the fence, found the bag right where it was said it'd be, and we went off to the safety of the Spillway to get drunk.

The Spillway was a concrete construction, sort of like a small dam, a few hundred feet from The Guy's house. Overflow water from the large pond across Big Bethel road flowed though it to drain away somewhere underground. At the sides of this sluice were broad cement slabs where one could sit or stand and watch the water happily splash away. We sat down in the semi-darkness, our backs to the rushing water, and we opened our sack.

More of the good stuff! This time a couple of 40s of high-quality premium foreign beer called Old English 800. For scale, these (40 oz.) bottles go for about 3 bucks today – so peel that back to 1981 or so, and Rock was making BANK at this gig. Also, for those of you who do not know, greatly inexpensive beer is *not* synonymous with *good* beer.

We sat, we drank, time went by at a normal pace, we got to the bottom of the bottles, looked at the label, looked at each other, and shrugged. Mind you, we were wrestlers; we had *very* fast metabolisms.

"What? Is that it?" asked Jeff derisively.

"This is bullshit," I countered, chucking my empty over my shoulder into the roiling maelstrom of the Spillway. "MAAAAANNNN." Then we made the typical rookie mistake. We both stood up rather quickly.

The woods spun around, I nearly went over backwards into the drink, Jeff grabbed me, pulled me back.

"Whoa," we said in unison, as the giggle juice hit our brains all at once. We looked at each other again, and started to laugh.

"THIS is wild," Jeff said, as we started to walk back toward the house lights of Bethel Manor, now wearing round-bottom shoes. We laughed, noting how enjoyable the feeling was, and how we sort of lost our motor control. We tried to walk straight lines and retain our composure because we knew we had to go home at some point and our parents might still be up.

As we were lurching around like normal dudes, me with my hands in my pockets, we failed to negotiate a storm drain grating that had the temerity to be completely flush with the level ground. We both stumbled awkwardly to the grass, laughing like idiots.

Only, my hands flew out of my pockets, along with the contents of said pockets, which included my house key.

Gone, gone in the night like a thing some drunken kid might lose while stumbling down a sidewalk in the dark. For a very brief time Jeff and I fumbled through the wet grass on our knees trying to find the key. Then one of us came up with a brilliant plan – we needed to get a flashlight. But from where?

"How about your house?" suggested Jeff, and immediately recanted when I reminded the dumbass that we were trying to find my house key.

"Hey, how about The Guy. His house is right there – he's always up?" he said pointing toward the house with a light in the window a few dozen yards away.

We stumbled to the window, tapped loudly, and soon The Guy opened his window, and puffed out a large cloud of smoke.

"Hey man, what's up," he cackled. "How'd you like your purchase?"

We explained that we were happy with our situation,

but that we also were in need of a flashlight to find my house key.

The Guy held up a finger and said he got us. He retreated into his room, we hear rummaging and noise, then he returned... with a tapered candle, which he held out the window triumphantly in his fist.

We asked him, quite rhetorically, what the fuck good is a candle, there's a soft breeze that will blow it out, and was he, in fact, a complete moron. He said no, "That's what this is for," and with his other hand he shoved a small tin of lighter fluid out at us.

Jesus Christ, all the stoner characters in movies are based on real people.

Being the stand up guy that The Guy was, he climbed out the window to help us, seeing as we were a very tiny bit skeptical of his plan. And just like that, two drunk teenagers and one stoned teenager were on their hands and knees in the wet grass trying to soak the wick of a church candle with lighter fluid so it would stay lit in the breeze to find a house key at 11pm at night.

And I will be an actual three-legged monkey's uncle if his plan didn't work.

"I told you man, I got you," he said, and strutted off back to his house, climbed back in the window, and slid the thing shut. Jeff and I just stood there staring at each other.

We showed up at my house a few minutes later, my mom was still up doing some work, I asked if it was okay that Jeff spent the night, 'cause we were really tired – not *drunk* or anything. She said fine. I flopped face down on my bed, Jeff sank into the bean bag chair in the corner, and we drifted off to sleep.

The next day, we were both visited by the gift that Old E Eight Oh Oh kept on giving – the gift of a painfully pounding headache that lasted all Sunday long, and perhaps a trip or two to the bathroom to look for Ralph and his friends Chuck and Bert.

Next day side effects aside, I was hooked. Beer and I became fast friends, and we went everywhere together, circumstances permitting. This was Virginia, and it already had a low drinking age at the time. At 18 you could drink on premise, say at a restaurant. At 19 you could buy beer at a 7-11 and take it home with you. The hard stuff you still had to be 21. I laugh, because wine was considered the hard stuff. *Wine* was lumped in with *Everclear*.

These fancy complicated laws aside – even if we knew they existed – there was a lot of drinking among the youth, because someone *always* had a friend named Rock, or Matty, or Boomer, or whatever. And also, quite frankly, there were a lot of convenience stores where they just didn't give a hoot to whom the beer was sold. If you looked old-ish enough, and had money, you could buy.

So when I drove back to my old High School stomping grounds the year after graduating, I was given a gift few folks get in their lives: the opportunity to bring the Circle of Life to its completion. Well, it being a Circle, I suppose I was just able to bring it back around for another go, but you catch my sentiment.

It was the summer of '83, and I had just finished my first semester of college at UNLV. I was doing stand-up in hotel lounges, I was drinking Michelob by choice, and most importantly, I knew the difference between the Michelobs and the Old English 800s of the world. I was a connoisseur.

Some friends and I were buying supplies for a little road trip up to Blacksburg to visit some friends at Virginia Tech, when we met some Sophomores from our Alma Mater in the parking lot.

They all looked like children; like 12-year-old urchin children, with their sooty faces, tattered clothes, and fingerless-gloved hands outstretched, asking us if we could *buy them beer*.

I had an urge to wave them off, telling these little kids that they needed to be in school, even though it was summer. I was an adult, I had to be responsible. I let them down easy

"I'd love to, but I ain't 21," I said, as I walked away toward the store. Mind you I was now living in Las Vegas, where everything was 21.

"No... you just need to be 19," one kid desperately shouted at me, reminding me, "they haven't changed the laws yet."*

I stopped in my tracks, turned and looked at these little day-care toddlers, with their big round, expectant,

---

*A year or so later the drinking age went back up to 21 for everything.

pleading Margaret Keane eyes. They certainly had the mien of some desperate high schoolers on a mission to get drunk for the first time... and I now had the opportunity to be *The Guy*.

I held out my hand, they plopped an abundance of money into it.

"Ah, you guys want the good stuff, I guess, huh?" I chuckled.

"Yeah man, thanks so much!" they could barely contain themselves.

"This ought to cover it. Wait here." I went into the store, met up with my friends, we got our supplies, and I went and got a case of beer. Check-out went super smooth, despite my being only 18, I guess I just had that worldly look on my face now that I was a college student. Or maybe the 18-year-old at the register just didn't give a shit. One way or the other, we left the store, my friends went to load our goodies into our car, and I went to meet the tots I had just bought alcohol for.

"Oh, man thanks!" they said, as they gingerly tucked the case of Miller into the trunk of their car, like it was Nitroglycerin.

"You guys take it easy," I said, as I jammed the rest of their change deep into my pocket. "Make it last."

Life Circled. Prophecy fulfilled. Another successful First Beer Memory created for three new initiates.

But on top of everything else... I made some *bank* on that deal.

TAXES AND DEATH

I have never been a fan of things that are needlessly convoluted and/or physically unbearable, even knowing their place in the world and their reason for being.

Taxes: waaaaayyy more convoluted and complicated than they need to be. I have no issues at all with paying taxes. You live in a society, shit needs to get done, taxes pay for that shit. But good God, it's absolutely ridiculous how difficult they have to make handing your money over to the government. Jesus Christ, just make it a flat tax. EVERYBODY, no matter how much you make, or your circumstances, just hand over 20% of what you made. I'd even be okay with 30%, but that's about the limit.

From that 25% (let's just find the middle there) the governments can take what they need to build roads, fund schools, make sure hospitals have band-aids and shrinks, and everyone's happy.

But no.

Instead, we got to answer questions about how married we are, and what time of day we cashed our checks, who was in the house when we bought that 65-inch High Def TV, do we want our children, and a barrage of other questions that are simply made to confuse and aggravate us before we hand over a huge chunk of our very hard-earned money.

And yet, if we make an *ungodly* amount of money, we don't end up paying much in taxes. You know the story, the tax burden is unevenly proportioned onto the folks with the least amount of income.

Needlessly.

Convoluted.

Las Vegas: so hot and dry you can die when the power goes out for fifteen minutes. You can not walk barefoot in Vegas, nor would you want to once you've seen what hits the ground in a city where it very rarely rains and washes off the sidewalks and parking lots, never even mind cooking the bottom of your feet.

Oh... and when it does rain? Well let's just hope you didn't park your car in Caesar's lot, because the water washes down into a ravine, and that is where your car now is. Because when it DOES rain in Vegas, it comes down in BARRELS. And it comes down HARD and fast, and then ten minutes after the entirety of Lake Mead falls back out of the sky, it has to go somewhere. And that's where the flash floods come in. And then you're just back to the insane heat.

Physically.

Unbearable.

These traits can be transferred to people as well. Interpersonal relationships can also be needlessly convoluted and physically unbearable. It ain't so bad when it's just a dating situation; i.e. you figure out that your new dating partner is too much work, you ditch them. I mean like, Vegan, but only with blue foods that willingly give themselves to be eaten? No.

They are physically incompatible, or their physicality is not something you care to deal with, say Type-A overly-hormoned hand-waving loud talkers... you split.

The further up the chain you go, however, the harder it can be to notice and relieve yourself of the complexities and physical bullshit.

By the time you get all the way up the ladder to the close, personal relationships of family, it can really do a job on you.

I have had a lot of people tell me over the years that family is family and you "have to" accept that. I, of course, always counter with

"Yeah yeah yeah, well HITLER was somebody's family member. Pol Pot had a wife and Kid. Nicolae Ceaușescu was a family man. Jim Jones and Charles Manson had families, and..."

"Okay, Greg, dial it back," they say, holding their palms up toward me, and backing away slowly to grab the tranq pistol we keep in the junk drawer, "that's overkill..."

"Yes. YES, it is overkill." I fire back, full well knowing it *was* a tad bit much... but also, really, *not*... point-making-wise. "They over-killed many people.... you think Hitler ever got a Father's Day card?"

Eyes would roll, shoulders would shrug, Jesus H Christs would get said, darts would get loaded into pistol chambers.

But I know I was right. Hitler never got a Father's Day card, until the day he died in Argentina at the age of 92.

Hitlerical history and theory aside, I know I go a bit overboard when it comes to this subject. In my family when we got pissed off at each other, we stopped talking to the offending family member, sometimes for decades. Not every family can do this, but we were wired that way. We were The Flying Wallendas of not speaking to each other.

It becomes needlessly convoluted and physically unbearable to keep up a relationship with someone who is supposed to be on your side but isn't. Or at the very least, they should treat you like a human being because you technically should be closer to them than almost anyone else in the world because they literally are the very first people you have ever met.

Such was the relationship I had with my father for most of my adult life. Or rather lack of relationship. I, like my dad's brother and his first two wives, chose not to deal with him after most of our interactions became tiresome, repetitive cliches.

Ridiculous behavior? Immature? I'll give you that; but I just got so tired, so quickly of his bludgeoning behavior where he not only never let you get a word in edgewise as he berated you, but he also just hammered you with the words he wanted you to say, ostensibly admitting he was right. Kind of like Don Logan, but not as funny. There is a reason three out of four of us children never really talked to Dad much throughout our lives.

The last time I saw my father in person before The Big Shunning, was a couple years after my wife and kids and I moved to Austin. He came driving through town on his way out to somewhere or back from somewhere. He didn't come by the house because the kids were sick, so I picked him up and we went to some restaurant.

It started well enough for the first few minutes, and then he started in on his bullshit of *why was I like the way I was*, and *why wasn't I getting a job that paid more*, and *why can't I just admit that I am wrong about absolutely everything*. After a few minutes of not being allowed to answer any of his rhetorical questions – I just slapped my knife and fork down on the table.

I was young, in a new town, in a new culture, with a wife and kids, and no, we were not particularly settled and comfortable yet, we were still sleeping on an air mattress at the time, but we were moving in the right direction. I *really* did not need this in a short visit from my father, but it *was* an even-odds expected outcome. Not once did he ask how the grandchildren were, not once did he ask how his daughter-in-law was.

"If you're not going to let me talk, Dad, why don't we

just stick to comments about the weather, huh?" I blurted out.

"This is what I'm talking about," he said, shaking his head in that deep, deep disappointment. "We can't even have a civilized conver..."

"Whelp, I think I'm done with lunch, let me get you back to your hotel." I stated as I stood up, and dropped my napkin on the table.

He was pissed, I could tell by the way his face looked, but also because I think he was always pissed at something, sooo, easy call there.

I dropped him off at his hotel, drove home, and just never bothered talking to him again. He in turn, never made any overtures to communicate with me either, until many years later.

My oldest brother and I frequently had a very short conversation about why I never talked to Dad. And I could never understand why my brother still visited and called Dad as often as he *did*, any more than he could understand why I *didn't*. It was a bit of a Hungarian stand-off, but it was what it was.

Somewhere nearing the twenty-year mark, might have been fifteen years, I really don't remember because I chose not to clock it. We'd infrequently get a card at Christmas time, or some family gift. My wife would tell me I should send him a card back, especially on his birthday, but I would not. It was *petty* as all get out, but I was not the only one in this ridiculous relationship.

He never acknowledged my birthday with a card,

he never acknowledged my high school graduation, he did not attend my wedding, he refused to acknowledge anything my wife and I found important, either in our lives or the lives of our kids. When asked to simply address cards to our kids – his grandchildren – using their hyphenated last name, he did not; so, I returned them, unopened, every time after the third offense.

Instead of learning, he just stopped sending. He pretty much never really acknowledged my wife existed at all in the later years, even when he was supposedly "loosening up;" cards or gifts were addressed to GREG DORCHAK, and the gifts, whatever they were, were me-based.

Meh.

Anyway, one year, around Father's Day, the year he was to turn 80, I was tearing out the walls in one of our bathrooms, this was not a metaphorical action, I was very literally tearing down the walls and rebuilding due to a leak.

As I sat there, screwing sheetrock to the studs in the bath stall, I started to think about all the times I had watched or helped my grandfather and my dad do the same in the old house we lived in up in Mohawk Lake.

Not entirely sure why, but I picked up the phone and called him, left a message saying I was remodeling a bathroom, and was just thinking about him. He called back a day or two later, we had a courteous chat, and a few months later, our son and I went up to celebrate Dad's 80th birthday, with my oldest brother and his wife.

My first time seeing Dad again, at 80, was a bit of an experience.

He was still large and imposing, but he was certainly slower, and had some health issues due to his days tromping around the Adirondacks for thirty years as a Forest Ranger.

We were polite to each other, I reintroduced him to his grandson who he had not seen since he was 6 months old. And the next two days were fine.

Then he started in again, albeit it to a bit lesser in degree. My brother and I would be talking about something, and Dad would barge in and cut us off and tell us we had the worst human thinking skills ever, and his chats in general got back to "My way or the highway" in tone; kind of short, terse non-listening sort of conversations.

My son caught up with me, away from the rest of the family, and whispered

"What the hell?"

I laughed and said

"Kid, you're not even getting him in his prime."

I told him to just let it roll off his shoulders, my Dad had never changed, and clearly was never going to. The visit was only a week, just hang out and let it go. He did, to his credit.

Over the next five years, Dad and I called each other maybe once a month or so, and had polite conversations. You still could never have any conversations with him where you had a dissimilar point of view, or difference in opinion, because you'd get the very stern growling – his bellowing was now dialed down to a 3 due to health issues – and he'd hang up on you if you didn't see things his way.

I just took it all with a grain of salt, smiled and clicked the red phone icon on my end. Some things never change. There was nothing to be gained.

The last couple years of Dad's life were marked by some infrequent trips to the hospital for different reasons, congestive heart failure being one. These infrequent trips grew more frequent, and in my head I knew it wasn't going to be much longer. But I had also learned to keep that shit to myself, because my wife has always told me I have a knack for killing people.

The end of November, maybe the beginning of December, Dad went into the hospital again. These trips had now come less than six months apart from the once-a-year they had been for a few years. I gave him a call in his room, and it started out okay.

Then, from his hospital bed, he made a mention of a book I had written, as he had just heard about it, very likely from my brother. I very specifically never mentioned the book to my father for this exact reason.

Dad started in on how little class I had... this simply from the TITLE of the book, which by today's standards is pretty subdued. He was literally judging a book by its cover. He was nothing if not consistent.

"Dad, the book wasn't written for someone like you, it was written for..." I started to explain

"It shows complete and utter lack of class, is what it shows." He growled. "Why can't you have a little class?"

I wasn't going to watch this show again, but I also wasn't going to fire back at him with a howitzer, it just wasn't worth it. I disagreed with him, tried to reason with him about demographics, culture, style, and marketing. But in the end, he hung on me.

About a month and half later he was in the hospital again, second week of February. He went in on Wednesday I think, had a rough few days, then rallied on Saturday. I talked to my brother on Friday, really wanted to tell him he should make the trip up there because I knew Dad wasn't going to live through the weekend. But I didn't say anything, I know what I do when I open my mouth.

Sunday morning I got the call from my brother, Dad had passed away a few hours earlier. Happily for Dad, he all but died alone in the rain like some sort of character out of a Hemingway novel. Except he was in the hospital and I think it was more like heavy wet snow. But I am pretty sure he timed it to happen before anyone was able to get in for visiting hours so he could actually be alone.

I have read a lot of memoirs and (auto)biographies about children of unbearably "complicated" parents, and the juicy details always played out similarly. How the parent was a monster, and the child was so relieved when they passed finally, and how "now I can live my life without the constant pressure and threat of doom looming over me. *Good riddance*."

I reflected on how the last thing my dad ever said to me was that I had absolutely no class whatsoever. Man, *that* was the stuff New York Times Best Sellers and

Hallmark movies were made from.

But the more I thought about it, the more I remembered something... which is the curse of a decent memory (I mean it was really only a month and a half ago).

When my father and I argued for that last time in December, and he tried his level best to squash me one more time, to shove his words down my throat for old time's sake, I was not letting him get to me.

"Well, I'm sorry you feel that way Dad, but you're wrong," I said matter-of-factly. There really wasn't any point at all in getting bent out of shape.

What I recalled (mind you, I really cringed to recall it) was the last thing he *actually* said to me before he hung up on me in the middle of that sentence. Albeit it was said with none of the positive emotion of the words in the phrase; it was said in that way someone says something when then don't *really* mean it, but they feel *obligated* to, like some sort of manifest compunction. What he actually said, derisively, right before he slammed the phone down – as best you CAN slam a smartphone down – was this:

"Yeah yeah yeah... love you." Click.

Actual last words spoken to me.

Wow.

What the hell was I supposed to do with THAT?

LIVE
MUSIC!
GIRLS!
GIRLS!
GIRLS!

Next to smells, music is one of the most powerful memory triggers. I get a whiff of ammonia any time, any where, and I am immediately transported back to a mid-spring chicken coop in Mohawk Lake, New York. Shoveling chicken shit that has been lovingly curated by a couple dozen egg-layers for the 6 months of winter. When I smell Gatorade, I am taken back to a 7-11 about a half mile from base housing in Tabb, Virginia, where – for a couple of bucks – one could get the classic Andy Capp Hot Fries and a bottle of green-flavored salt water.

When I hear *Bohemian Rhapsody*, I am suddenly 10 years old, under the blankets at midnight, catching a radio wave out of NYC on my 7-dollar transistor radio.

Vivid, instant memories that never seem to shrivel with age. *That* smell or *that* song brings them back to life *in an instant*.

And now, thanks to the advanced age of those like me, and the bullshit never-ending advance of the construct known as time, radio stations are now mixing into their current hits play lists a lot of "Oldies," from WAAAAYYYYYYY back when. Like Blondie, The Cars, Psychedelic Furs. Really old stuff.

I'll be driving down the highway in the modern times of 2024, minding my own business, being a viable and productive member of society, when some jackass DJ comes on and says something hip and happening like

"And here's another blast from the past! Where were YOU when THIS song came out in 1979?"

A quick math check in my head confirms that 1979 was indeed 20 years ago, as The Pretenders' *Brass in Pocket* starts to play. I start grooving, remembering seeing the video when it first appeared on MTV; being madly in love with Chrissie Hynde, which was not easy, because I was also in love with Debbie Harry and I had no idea how to handle that situation.

I knew I could only love *one* of them at a time, but there was still some room in there for a possible *compromise*, as this was the 80s and things happened, miracles occurred. I held onto hope.

Anyway, about the time things are getting good in my head, the song ends and that Dick-Jerk comes back on says

"That was *Brass in Pocket* by the Pretenders, reaching back almost 45 years into the vault of..."

WHAT???!!

FORTY-FIVE YEARS?

NO.

I was in High School when that came out.

That was only... lemmee see... borrow one from the 2, borrow again from the 10... HOLY SHIT.

The realization sets in, some brain cells writhe in pain, my youthful exuberance fizzles, and I slow the car down and flip on a blinker. Any blinker. Doesn't matter. Soon, there is a line of cars honking behind me all the way to the Walmart, where I lacklusterally grab a cart from the guy about my age in a Rascal(tm) Scooter who greets me at the door; we exchange "hot enough for ya's?!"

I shuffle in my house slippers behind a cart with three good wheels as I trudge up and down the aisles to find my Boost Nutritional Supplement, which is the only item I can remember from the list of things I was supposed to get. I didn't bring my Dollar Store reading glasses, so I can't make out the rest of the list in my hand. Despite the fact that the Nutrient Boost Drink has always been in exactly the same place for ten years, I check every aisle in the store in case it has moved.

It has not, as the last place I checked will attest.

Then, as I stand there in the check-out line waiting for the ONE solitary, personed check-out, because F U I'm gonna use self-check that has 38 stations open, everything inside of me just sort of... quietly... dies...

The cute young lady at the checkout scans my case of Boost Supplementing Drink, awww shhhhhhoot, that's not strawberry. I was sposda get strawberry. Well I ain't walking all the way back there and exchanging it. Check-out lady throws a quick smile my way, and I know exactly what that smile means now.

"Awww, look at the grandpa, trying to hold onto one last shred of humanity with a short burst of energy so he can spend some quality time with his grandchildren before he dies."

After limping both physically and mentally back to my car, muttering under my breath about these young whipper-snappers today, and telling them that I, too, used to be a vibrant, active youth with dreams and desires of my own, I chuck the Supplemental Boost Nutrients Shake Drink in the back of my car, and leave the cart bumped against the median in the lot.

"You're so f-in' youthful, YOU take it to the convenient cart return chute," I grumble.

Before pulling out of the parking lot in my Edsel, I find the "Oldies Station" on the radio, for no other reason than because it is *formatted* as a station that already plays all the "Old Stuff," meaning I don't have to listen to some smug 30-year-old prick call out the YEAR it came out, or how many YEARS it has been since it came out, or how OLD I have to be if I remember it coming out. Just pure gold, playing back to back good ol' Rock and Roll from ten years ago when I was young.

I feel the life starting to squish back into my body as Blondie wails

"When... I met you in the restaurant..."

And I think of the first time I arrived in Virginia Beach with my friend Mark. Windows open, salty warm sea air blowing through the matte gold Chevy Nova. We found a parking spot behind an arcade, and spent the first few hours of our day at the beach inside a dark cave showing off our Galaga skills, and getting noticed by some cute girls we would see again later on the actual sand. It ultimately led nowhere, but we had fun chatting them up in our OP and IZOD fashions. I was OP. Mark was totally into the alligator.

Easy by The Commodores comes on at some point before I'm even done remembering the time at Virginia Beach, and there I go, back to my first time at a high school dance. I'm a little buzzed, and I'm dancing with a girl I fell for kinda hard, but never asked out because I was in the middle of a *Thing*. It was a *real* Thing, mind you, nothing *made up,* or *only in my hamster-wheel-powered head*, and it certainly wasn't in any way the *absolute dumbest* reason on the *planet*.

> (See, what happened was, I had already
> asked out a few girls, all of whom said
> thank you no, even when I was certain I
> read the signs correctly. I could not stand
> the thought of rejection from this girl, so I
> never asked her out.

*She made me laugh, and she had a
great laugh. I literally sat and listened
to her read a phone book one time in the
empty cafeteria. I have no idea why we
were there, may have been a theater thing,
and we were on break. But we took it into
our heads to see how funny we both could
be if all we did was read from the phone
book.*

*I looked up at her smile, that black hair
just all over the place, all contrasty and shit
on that shiny, copper-colored blouse. And
that's when I knew, I knew I could not go
to any more school dances. If I didn't go to
where she was, I wouldn't have to deal with
her, and thus endure the pain of another
NO.)*

I told you, it wasn't stupid, it was an *actual* Thing that
I had figured out using reasoning and the problem-solving
skills of an adult.

So what I did was (points to noggin) I went to dances
at *other* high schools. And there, I stood against the wall
and watched everyone having fun from afar, as far as afar
went in a high school cafeteria. Or sometimes I would
talk to the parents of friends of mine, whom I knew from
wrestling. I could see the look on their faces as they tried
to chaperone the other couple hundred kids they were
charged with

"Why is this kid sitting here talking with me, there are

girls everywhere. What, is he hiding from some other girl at his high school. THAT'S pretty immature," they clearly mused.

About the time that even I was figuring out that this behavior *might have been weird*, The Commodores came back on, and once again *Easy* filled the air. And just as I was about to think about Her, I got a tap on my shoulder. No, it wasn't *that* awesome, but it was awesome enough.

It was some *other* girl, cute as all get out, big ol' square-framed glasses framed by hair that parted in the middle, dropped down both sides of the face and curled in just under the chin.

"Hi. Would you like to dance?" she asked in a quiet confidence that immediately had me.

"Ummm, YEAH..." I said, and followed her to a spot on the floor. I could almost hear the eyes of that Chaperone roll skyward as she whispered "*Thank you GOD.*"

I danced with that girl for a few songs. I liked her, I know now she very probably liked me. And then nature took its course... which is code for I left without getting her name or number, or telling her mine, and I went home.

Within the Pantheon of Those Who Got Game, I was right up there with the greats like Duckie, Rick Blaine, and Quasimodo.

I saw Mystery Girl at least one more time, under similar circumstances, only the song was *Sometimes When We Touch* by Dan Hill. Again with the tap on my shoulder, again with the polite request in confidence. Again, a few dances that made my night, and frightened me even more.

How long could I get away without asking her name? Why wasn't she asking mine? But she is asking me to dance... soooo... right? RIGHT? *Why is shit so friggin' complicated?*

How hard, exactly, is it for the girl to just *say the words* to let a guy know they are actually interested (like it mattered... I fucked that one up too once)? I know now what the reality was, the onus was on me.

But I had been burned way too often, and was *way too dumb* and inexperienced to begin with. As a result, I was frozen in a glacier of self-doubt and inaction that caused me to miss out on a lot of fun with some great girls. Instead, I was relegating myself to an ever-thickening bubble of insecurity and confusion that would insulate me for a lot of years. Never letting them in, never letting me out.

I was okay with that. I was a rock, I was an island... and a rock feels no pain.

As it turned out, that philosophy didn't last long, maybe four years – only into my second year of college. Though I must say, I turned it into a bit of art, that pushing girls – then young women – away as easily as I breathed.

In college I worked up the nerve to ask one or two young ladies out, thinking well, new school, new state, new lifestyle... a fresh start. You know how it started?

I'll bet you can guess. It started with a couple more "No thank you's." Which reinforced my little Bubble of Solitude.

Then I started working at the student newspaper at UNLV, and by osmosis, or perhaps leakage, also the student radio station, which was on the same balcony office suite in the student union; we shared a wall between us.

I had gotten my FCC card but only worked as a fill-in DJ, because they were full up at the moment. But when any of them had to take a break, or go grab something from their Green Man, I would sit in. I was spinning the wax – *did that sound hip* – one night as the regular DJ, my buddy Romney – who was trip in and of himself – had to make a run.

I just started up a favorite song of mine that I was introduced to by the Alt-Rock play list at KUNV: *Madame Butterfly* by Malcolm McLaren. In walked this DJ who I thought was particularly attractive.

I never had a chance to talk to her or even see her up close before, so I was kinda caught off guard when she walked in, her fuchsia undercut freshly gelled or moussed or whatever it is you do with an undercut, her torn denim-based outfit a little extra revealing tonight.

"What's up," she chinned me.

"Not much," I chinned back.

"Good call, I love this song," she said as she hung up her book bag.

"Yeah, I know," I thought to myself, "I first heard it one night when you played it on your shift."

We got to talking, and eventually started to hang out on the balcony overlooking the Food Court two floors below us, talking about music, movies, shit in general. She, I thought in my naive inexperienced mind, was pretty worldly and mature and I totally had the hots for her. Which meant one thing: there was no way in HELL I was going to ask her out.

She didn't seem to mind much, although at the same time seemed to enjoy my company. She eventually got a gig working as a VJ for a sort of local version of MTV in Las Vegas, and invited me to a musical event they hosted one Friday night just up the road on Maryland Parkway and Flamingo Blvd., one of those restaurant/bar type places.

She laughed and sauntered over when I got pinged at the door for being underage, she whispered something to the bouncer and he let me in.

"Be cool, man," he said just loud enough for me to hear as I passed him, his eyes never looking at me.

Be cool? Are you serious? Why was everybody so concerned with my level of coolness? Did I have some neon sign Damoclesing itself above me buzzing "NOT COOL?" I was as cool as they came.

Kiss my ass, "*Be Cool.*" YOU be cool. Jerk.

I had one beer that was snuck out to me by a friend I met there, when Fuchsia Undercut came up to me on the patio.

"What the hell are you drinking, man?" she said as she took the bottle out of my hand, polished it off and set the empty down on the railing. "Hey, Ron, you know Greg? He works at the student newspaper and radio station." She waved over another friend of hers who worked at the video music station, and we started talking.

Ron happened to be drinking something in a highball glass, looked a lot like ice tea.

"What's that," I asked, like some podunk farmer kid, pointing at the glass like I had just seen some sort of kangaroo for the first time. My knowledge of mixed cocktails at that moment in history was beer, Screwdriver, Harvey Wallbanger. End of list.

"Long Island Ice Tea," Ron said, "want to try it?"

He shoved the drink at me, I took a sip.

"Yes please," I shot back.

Fuchsia Undercut laughed an evil laugh.

"Awww shit," she rolled her eyes, smiling "they ain't gonna give you one of THOSE at the bar. Hang on, I know the bartender." Of course she did.

Ron and I talked some more as she left to get my drink. He asked me a lot of questions about how I knew Undercut, and how long have I worked with her, and what was my major and so forth.

Before I knew it Undercut swooshed back around the corner of the bar, just as the Psychedelic Furs' *Heaven* cued up on the sound system. She sauntered toward me with a freakin' milkshake-sized glass in her hand, the ice cubes clicking around the straw. Yes, the whole thing was in hyper-real slow-mo until she reached me and held the drink out.

"There you go, man, I had him make it a double so you didn't need to go back for more."

The twinkle in her eye as she winked should have been a dead giveaway that shit was about to go down. Ron looked at me funny

"You ever *have* a Long Island Iced Tea before?" he asked, a slight look of concern on his face.

"No, but they taste great," I offered like a complete dumbass, slurping away like a truly blissfully ignorant noob.

I do not recall much more of that night. The romantic in me believes I did indeed "be cooled" as the bouncer asked. I did drive home. And I did have somewhat of a screaming headache the next day. I also did never drink that much Long Island Iced Tea in one sitting again.

Nothing of any note-worthiness every happened with Undercut. I mean I liked her enough, but she clearly had a much more healthy appetite for relationships than I was going to be able to take care of. She frightened me in a whole different way than most other girls or young women I had liked heretofore. But I enjoyed the time, and frequently called in to get her to play the *Heaven* video on the local music channel.

The very last music/girl connection I ever needed though, happened about a year or so later. Out front of the Moyer Student Union on the UNLV campus, there was a turning circle where you could pull in and drop folks off, or unload whatever it was that needed to go into the Union. Long term parking it was not. As newspaper staff, we soundly ignored that rule most days, especially after hours.

I was somewhat seeing this young woman I met a few months before, she was the sister of a guy I worked at the newspaper and radio station with. I say "somewhat seeing," because well, by now it should have been pretty obvious what my dating prowess was like. I was chest deep in avoidance at all costs – most very especially when I really liked the person, but didn't want to screw it the hell up by making the first, awkward move. By making *any* move at all, even when faced with irrefutable evidence that I would have been correct.

On this chilly October night we were out driving around in my little red Mustang, and I had to drop her back off at the newspaper because I had other things to do. We sat there in the 15-minute parking area in front of the student union for way more than 15 minutes, talking that stupid meaningless small talk people do when all the subtext is really *"oh my god, would you make a move already?"*

I clearly was NOT going to. We've been over this already. Duh. Leave me alone.

I was just about ready to forcibly shove her out the door, when Jim Croce came on the radio. *Time In A Bottle*. The first few lines drifted out of the speakers, she moved in, and the next thing I know we're kissing. For *me*, at least, that kind of kiss that blanks your mind, you're no longer aware of anything else, what day it is, where you're parked. Your own name.

It was pretty damn fantastic.

And then we had to part, she had to get up to the office to work, I had to go do something stupid that in no way measured up to what just happened. Pretty much Greg 101 stuff.

I drove off on Cloud Nine Hundred. I immediately had the station preset button in my head lock in that song, and that moment, and that young woman, and I have played that one over in my head I cannot count how many times in the 40 years we've been married. I had a stupid smile stapled to my face almost all the way to my next stop.

As I pulled into the parking lot of whatever dive I was going to listen to my friends in the band, the smile left my face as I stared out the driver's side window into space. Dreaming. Dreaming is free... DREEEEAAAAMING...

"Hmm," I mused after a period of time, "*definitely* going to have to tell her boyfriend at some point."

WHAT HAPPENED IN VEGAS?

At 17 I found myself in an honest-to-God city. In the fall of 1982, Las Vegas had a population of around 500 thousand, while Newport News (the closest "big city" to me in Virginia) topped out at maybe 150k. Both experiencing single-digit population growth for some time.

Pretty big change for a kid who grew up in the BFE of upstate New York. Geographically, they were just about as far away from each other as you could get and still be in the continental United States. Culturally, they were on different planets in different star systems... as far as I was concerned.

When tallying average light-bulb usage alone, Newport News wasn't even on the same map as Sin City.

MY GOD, just brightly colored lights EVERYWHERE. The strip was one thing, because there was a (relatively) good amount of space between casinos there; but then you drove down Fremont Street, and all the buildings were right up against each other, it was just an ocean of lights.

Pretty overwhelming for someone who just a few years ago was uncontrollably giddy because they installed a streetlight on the road in front of his house.

And then the gambling hit you. I think the one thing most people do not expect when they first step into a casino, is the noise. That WALL of

DING DING DING DING DING DING

BLOOOOOO-OOP BLOOOOOOOOO-OOP

CAKITTA CACKITTA CACKITTA CACKITTA

Not even to mention the sounds of human beings talking, complaining, laughing, drinking, praying, and whatnot. I don't know what others thought when first entering a casino in the gambling Mecca of the USA, but it sure threw me for a loop. Not everyone gambling is happy and festive, or even dressed in a tuxedo and ordering vodka martinis shaken OR stirred.

There are a lot of folks who are desperate and unhappy mixed in with the milieu. Going to Vegas is NOT what you want to do as a financial retirement plan, or even as a New Business Start-Up Plan. However, if your plan is simply to lose all your money and get drunk, Thumbs up, Grand Choice!

Think Late Night Walmart Run, then add craps tables and slot machines and free drinks... now you're getting closer.

Man, it was a lot to process.

The first casino I ever stepped into was my mom and stepdad's favorite on the corner of Sahara and Las Vegas Boulevard (The Strip). It was called The El Rancho, and it was the child of the original that opened in 1948 just across the street. The NEW! El Rancho opened maybe a month or two before I got to Vegas... so it still had that New Crushed Dreams Smell to it.

Of course, I was not allowed to *technically* be in casinos at the age of 17, and I *certainly* was not allowed to gamble. If I were ever found to have shoved a few nickels into a slot machine that was in an under-visited corner of the gambling floor, and was able to parley that 45 cents into over a hundred dollars worth of nickels, that would have been grounds for extreme measures.

If someone ever did that, why, they'd probably have to scoop those 2000 nickels (no digital or ticketed pay-outs back then) into a giant paper popcorn-type super-cup and slip out to the car and leave the grounds immediately. Fortunately, I had a Big Boy beard* to cover my age, and it was a bit of a walk from Security's video monitoring room to where I was.

---

*It was patchy and barely what could even legally pass for a "beard."

Slot machines, poker machines... even back then you simply could not avoid them, they were everywhere, and I mean in the airport, the supermarkets and even a few bathrooms. Though I could honestly sort of get behind the idea of slot machines or a Keno Lounge in a bathroom, I mean I play old-school Tetris until my thighs are numb anyway, why not have a chance at winning a fortune while you take a shit?

Regardless, Vegas would GET. YOUR. MONEY.

Which is the thing that the locals would learn very quickly. *Visiting* Vegas and *Living* in Vegas were two very different animals. The shine wore off that 700-megawatt apple rather quickly, and you settled into a fairly nice existence, one in which everything was open 24 hours a day, entertainment was everywhere and fairly inexpensive, and a breakfast of steak, eggs and lobster tail was just $4.99.

This was a pretty fine place to spend some time as an exiting teen/entering young adult.

One thing that took my notice, as one might imagine, was the live stage shows. You hear a lot about them, maybe see a few reenacted in movies or plays, but seeing one live was an experience. I know I was not exactly the prime demographic for this sort of thing, but I honestly was left scratching my head after my first full-blown Las Vegas Review with Dancing Girls (women).

Here's the thing, you sat in these nice seats, maybe at a table, with a meal and drinks (no drinks for me, not old enough), and then the Emcee came out, blah blah blah, then finally "here's some girls in heels and plumes!"

And these fairly from-a-distance-in-the-right-lighting-nice-looking women came out, in heel sand plumes, lots of sequins, HUGE toothy SMILES!, arms around each other, step-kick-step, one end of the stage to the other, upstage to downstage, moving as one, never losing their perfectly-chiropracted composure.

Then at one point, I can't even remember what triggered the transition, maybe it was 9pm, when perhaps all the kids would be home (or in the room) asleep? Anyway, at some point, the Fancy Ladies went backstage. Emcee came back out, blah blah blah for a bit, and then "And heeeeeere's those girls in heels and plumes one more time!" And yes, they came right back out, step-kick-step, SMILES!, twist-and-turn, upstage, downstage, left and right.

But this time you could see their tits.

I thought it might be a bit more exciting, you know, live boobs on stage and all. But it left me completely deficient in the pluss department. It was, for all intents and purposes, exactly the same routine, maybe different music... just way more nippled than before.

What exactly was the *point*? And I was a *teenaged male,* mind you. Oh my god... was... was I a *boor*?

I don't know what I *thought* I was expecting, but it certainly wasn't this ridiculous display of unimaginative stage work. I was thinking maybe something that might cause me embarrassment, what with my mother and stepfather at the table... plus three other complete strangers. But I had no discernible reaction to whatever *this* was. In fact, it bored me.

So yeah, the shine wore off quickly, and I just got into the rhythm of living.

The nature of the city was fun frequently though, especially as a college student. Sure, the Hotel Business College at UNLV was one of the best in the country, what with an entire city to draw from for lesson plans, but even the other activities on campus benefitted from the type of city it was.

Did you know, that even being teenagers, students could, if motivated, hire strippers and send them into a student council meeting to disrupt proceedings? And did you further know that you could do it twice? And maybe also use newspaper funds to pay for said strippers, disguising it all as research for a news story? Or... or... wherever it was the customer worked at, newspaper was an example I made up.

And if One actually DID work at the student newspaper, there were all sorts of legal, sanctioned, age-appropriate things that could be done. Like tagging along with an entertainment writer when they went to review a stage show such as the comedy showcases at the Dunes or Stardust hotels. Where you could Plus-One yourself into famous comics' dressing rooms and sit through the interviews, or meet George Carlin, who was standing at the back of the house, right behind your seats watching an up-and-coming comic do their set.

The fun never ended.

Even a normal errand, such as taking your friend to the airport, could be an adventurous event. Using a University vehicle, you could pick up your friend and drive them right to the front door of the airport in the Red Zone, and not be questioned too much.

And let's say this friend, who was deathly afraid of flying, had doubled-down on his already double-dose of valium prescribed by Dr. Feelgood from that "clinic" over on Charleston Boulevard. If you had to physically manhandle him through the doors, down the concourse like a human sized blob of Silly Putty, and pour him into his seat on the plane, then strap him in so he couldn't leave... you could... and nobody took notice.

It was official University Business. And the nineteen-year-old and seventeen-year-old doing all that nonsense were not questioned. That was their job. Clearly. Decals on the truck, man.

Everyone in that city had their side-hustles, too, even the irresponsible teenagers that worked at the 24-hour Kinko's across the street were able to have a pretty decent side-gig making "replications" of things that may have been officially printed... for purely entertainment purposes. Remember, it was the early 80s, so there weren't any home computer systems yet.

However, if some employee also happened to work at, let's say for the sake of argument... a newspaper office, they might could have some typesetting done, then use their considerable layout and design skills to create a fun little harmless document for fun for others who needed a fun little document or card for reasons of research or drinking fun, or whatever.

Having a 24-hour city was also a huge boon to college students in the market for work, and the sheer magnitude of jobs and shifts available made for some nice bennies when a friend was able to secure employment at a coveted job. Sometimes that job was as simple as cashier at the Food Lion just off campus. Food Lion took all competitor's coupons, which is how they managed to take some business away from the Vons and Smith's of the city.

One of the writers/editors at the newspaper got a job cashiering at the Food Lion, and was telling this young couple – that was expecting their first child – about the rather lax practice of accepting competitors' coupons. This was also in the days before digitization and beepers that scanned the bar codes on items. Coupons were entered by hand, presumably cross-checked by the cashier.

The two parents-to-be, being really short on funds, but a bit blessed with the scheming genes, devised a plan with the Check-Outist. Diapers, formula, all sorts of baby's needs, maybe even some steaks on the weekends could be purchased at a discount with this clever coupon policy. Coupons that did not always match the purchases made. And it was a fun run for those nameless people involved while it lasted.

But all good things must end, and so did this weekend Food Lion run, when one night there may have been a few too many coupons clipped and handed over, and this over-exuberance of coupon usage... may have resulted in the Food Lion having to give some amount of money back as change to the young couple – even though no money had initially been offered to the checker.

A split second of exchanging furtive glances between the three, not knowing what to do, led to change being given, groceries being quickly and silently packed, and then the check-out technician quitting that job at the end of the shift as a preemptive measure.

Knowing when to walk away from the table in Vegas is half the battle. You get a huge stack of chips after splitting and doubling down (where available) on Aces in Blackjack... you cash out.

The three friends refrained from making any further verbal or eye contact as they all, quickly – but calmly – took different exits from the discount grocery store, promising to never again speak of this event until a reasonable amount of time had passed.

After all, what HAPPENS in Food Lion... STAYS in Food Lion.

ABOUT THE AUTHOR

Greg Dorchak was born in Portsmouth, VA, and grew up in The Adirondacks of New York State. He returned to the Tidewater Region with his mother after his parents divorced. In High School, he wrestled, acted in plays, and was named Class Clown.

He performed stand-up and improv while living in Las Vegas, where he attended UNLV working on a filmmaking degree.

An actor, writer, artist, and filmmaker, he wrote and directed the award-winning feature-length film *Kopy Kings*, a workplace comedy about the misfits at a 24-hour copy center.

Dorchak lives in Austin with his wife. He paints whimsical art for the average person, putters, and enjoys working on his car every now and again.

Light bulbs trigger him something wicked.